HEALING OF MEMORIES

Healing of Memories

by
Matthew Linn, S.J.
and
Dennis Linn, S.J.

PAULIST PRESS
New York / Paramus / Toronto

IMPRIMI POTEST:
Leo F. Weber, S.J.
Provincial, Missouri Province
July 22, 1974

Library of Congress
Catalog Card Number: 74-17697

ISBN: 0-8091-1854-8

Published by Paulist Press
Editorial Office: 1865 Broadway, N.Y., N.Y. 10023
Business Office: 400 Sette Drive, Paramus, N.J. 07652

Printed and bound in the
United States of America

Contents

Foreword

With the extraordinary expansion of the ministry of healing-through-prayer among the churches in these past few years, I have also seen a marvelous diversity of ways of praying begin to develop. It's as if God were teaching different people and groups the particular ways they can best minister healing to the sick. The way that Kathryn Kuhlman prays is not the same as the way that Barbara Shlemon prays; the way that Kenneth Hagin prays is not the way that Father Mike Scanlan prays— their methods of prayer are as different as their personalities. Furthermore, some people endowed with the ministry of healing find that God seems to help them in praying for certain special kinds of sickness; Michael Gaydos, for example, seems to have a special ministry of praying for those with eye problems.

A good deal of my work then has been not only in encouraging Christians to exercise their happy privilege of praying for the sick and to learn the basic principles of healing prayer, but also in helping people to listen to the Spirit and to discover that particular way in which God is calling them to pray. Here in St. Louis many of my friends have taken up the challenge of praying for the sick and have then proceeded to apply it in an individual way to their own areas of ministry.

Among these friends we (at Merton House) are happy to count the Jesuits who live, as we do, in old houses in the Central West End and combine a life of study at St. Louis University with an active ministry to the disadvantaged. Prominent among these friends and co-laborers are Fathers Matt and Denny Linn, who, until recently, lived just several doors down the street and who spend the summers working in the Dakotas among the Sioux Indians. Once Matt and Denny became involved in the charismatic renewal, they soon recognized the importance of prayer for "healing of memories" in their own ministry.

Taking the concept of healing of memories (described by Mrs. Agnes Sanford in *The Healing Gifts of the Spirit*, Lippincott, 1966) and developing it in their own way as they gave directed retreats and spiritual direction, they have discovered new insights into the applications of prayer for inner healing. In this book they share their experience in an area of prayer where we are continually making new discoveries as to how the Lord wants his people to grow into that perfect freedom given by the Spirit.

What Matt and Denny have found is that there are many Catholics who want to make their reception of the sacrament of reconciliation (penance) more meaningful. In particular, those Catholic charismatics who have read Father Michael Scanlan's books *Power in Penance* (Ave Maria Press, 1972) and *Inner Healing* (Paulist Press, 1974) and who yearn to receive the sacrament in that in-depth way say that they are unable to find confessors who know how to combine confessions of sins with prayer for inner healing. This sacramental need is at the heart of the pastoral problem addressed by Fathers Matt and Denny who describe how individuals can prepare themselves for a meaningful reception of penance or can learn to pray for themselves and bring healing to the past. They have discovered insights in two particularly valuable areas:

1. in becoming *forgiving*: getting rid of bitterness and the roots of sickness in order to live free from the wounds of the past;

2. to see the past *in a new, positive light*: Christ can help us to see the beneficial aspects of personal hurts so that we can thank God in all things rather than see only the dark side of the past.

In concentrating on these aspects of inner healing, the authors leave aside other areas of healing that I have found important in praying with those suffering as a result of past hurts. Among these aspects they choose not to concentrate on are:

1. Praying *with* people, when this is possible. Often, this praying one to one or in a small team seems to be the most beneficial way.

2. The person's trying to forgive or trying to see things in a new light is not always enough. The *direct healing power* of Jesus Christ, applied by prayer, is often needed in order that the person wounded by the past be able to forgive, or to see in a new light, or to be healed of past hurts. Healing of memories is more than a psychological process of "talking it out" or a re-education of old thought-patterns (although all these may be involved). I find that there is a real power in prayer, beyond any human input. This power comes largely from a direct empowering by Christ and is not to be compared to that healing effected by medicine men or human means.

Most particularly, I am grateful to Matt and Denny for delving so deeply into the need for forgiving our enemies and for discovering ways of helping us to follow this most difficult and most necessary of Jesus' requirements in order that we might form the kind of loving community he desires.

Francis S. MacNutt, O.P.
Merton House
St. Louis, Mo.

I
Power To Heal

Imagine your whole body perspiring and the air heavy to breathe. You are sharing the Sioux sweat lodge ceremony, a rite of thanksgiving and forgiveness.[1] In the center of an igloo-style lodge rest fourteen red hot rocks upon which the medicine man has just thrown water. The hot steam penetrates your entire body. Your whole body feels like bare feet standing on sun-beaten pavement.

As sweat oozes from your body, the medicine man thanks God for four-legged animals, the winged peoples and two-legged non-wingeds. You hear often the words that end most Sioux prayers and have power to open up the sweat lodge door: *Mitakuye oyasin* ("With all beings and all things let us be relatives"). After thanking God for relatives, you pray with the medicine man for his neighbors who quarrel, for his estranged son, and for the government and Indian people quarreling at Wounded Knee.

After you all have thanked God for your relatives and asked forgiveness for ways in which you have strained that friendship, you begin to blow on the person next to you. You feel cool air coming across a special part of your body. If you are suffering from a headache, you feel the cool air around your head; if

1

from depression, then around your heart; or if from fear to speak, then around your lips. The refreshing cool breeze symbolizes the idea that forgiveness heals.

Five years ago when I first participated in the sweat bath, I thought that a person would be healed very rarely. It's just one of those primitive superstitions, I told myself. Now having worked as a therapist in a psychiatric clinic, and having directed retreats and workshops, I would be amazed if this rite of forgiveness did not heal everyone either physically, mentally or spiritually. I have seen people shuffle into the psychiatric clinic with long lists of physical symptoms which evaporate one by one as they begin to forgive their parents. I have witnessed many retreatants responding to God's call in ways they never dreamed after they forgave themselves, their neighbor or God. Especially during the past five years, the Lord has shouted clearly to me that forgiveness brings healing.

Yet, how many times do we plead for forgiveness, whether in confession or in prayer, but things do not change? We are no more open to our better self, God, or our neighbor than when we began. The headaches, periods of depression or fear to speak out still grip us and choke out life.

How do we know whether God wants us to ask for healing or to stay weak so that He can draw us closer to Himself? The answer lies in discerning whether the weakness, illness etc., is making us God-centered and neighbor-centered or more narrowly self-centered. If we are growing more self-centered, then this indicates that God wants to work a healing.

For example, a crippled friend calls day and night in a demanding tone that the world should wait on her. God yearns to heal such self-centeredness. But I doubt if God yearns so to heal a fellow Jesuit whose blindness sensitizes him to hear twice as much. Such listening makes him an outstanding spiritual director who can experientially share how God takes our hand and guides us in the midst of darkness. Christ may keep him blind because He works through the blindness.

Christianity is not painless but a call to share in the suffering of Christ. We too should undergo the pain of not communicating His love just as He wept over Jerusalem or the flight of His chosen twelve. If we preach His word, we too will suffer. We will be ignored, hated, and will find no place to lay our head (Mt 10:16; Jn 15:18). We do not pray to be delivered from this suffering but to become less self-centered and more Christ-centered.

But is it not part of normal Christian living to want to act one way and yet find ourselves doing the opposite? We want to open ourselves, to share our lives, yet we find ourselves closed off, living individualistically. We are pulled like Paul before his conversion, "I find myself doing the very thing I hate" (Rom 7:15).

Paul is not focusing on the way a Christian should experience himself. Rather, he role-plays the way a person feels powerless when he lives by law and not by the Holy Spirit. Chapter 8 of Romans portrays how a Christian should experience himself. It speaks in terms of a new creation, a man dead to sin, a free man. This freedom requires the Spirit because law reveals only wrongdoing, but the Spirit injects inward strength to correct the wrong.

So then, my brothers, there is no necessity to obey our unspiritual selves or to live unspiritual lives. If you do

live in that way, you are doomed to die; but if by the
Spirit you put an end to the misdeeds of the body, you
will live (Rom 8:12).

By becoming a human being, we begin acting in
self-centered ways. By becoming a Christian we give
ourselves to Christ to liberate us from our sinfulness by
the power of His Holy Spirit. When Christ challenges
us with the great commandments to love God and
neighbor, He is not like a master asking the impossible
by dangling a bone three feet beyond a chained dog.
Publicans and prostitutes, Peter and the good thief tes-
tify loudly with many others that Christ's healing forgiveness transforms them to love God, neighbor and
self as Christ called them to do.

Pneuma in Greek means not only "spirit" but also
"wind," "breath," and "air." For the Sioux, the
pneuma felt around your head, heart, or mouth expresses *Wakantanka's* (the Great Mystery's) healing power.
For the Christian the Father sends the *pneuma* to
endow us with new life, to make us new creations. For
both the Sioux and Christian, forgiveness instills the
healing *pneuma*. Frequently, however, the Christian experiences no healing. How can we celebrate the sacrament of penance to experience healing, a new creation,
a person visibly changed like the good thief or Peter? A
process called healing of memories prepares us for the
sacrament of penance and the deeper forgiveness that
heals.[2]

Discussion Questions

(*Note:* The discussion questions are to stimulate
thought and often may not have a simple answer.)

1. Did Christ always heal those who asked?

2. Should a Christian experience this: "I find myself doing the very thing I hate" (Rom 7:15)?

3. How do you think confession could become more of a healing experience?

II
Healing of Memories:
What Is Involved?

Last year, after a busy week's work at a psychiatric clinic, I went off to rest and make a retreat. One question asked during the retreat was: "When did you feel closest to God?" People answered with times when a friend died, or when lonely, or when unjustly blamed. It came as a shock because experiences that brought these people closer to God sounded so much like experiences that brought my patients to the psychiatric clinic.

I became aware that we could take every moment in two ways: one, it could open us to God, our neighbor and ourself; or two, it could close us to the point of needing psychiatric help. Death of a close friend, for instance, could make us forever angry at God. Pain of separation could keep us from ever opening ourselves deeply to another person. On the other hand, death could provide the loneliness filled only by a deepening personal relationship with God. Death could also give us a new appreciation of our life and a desire to share it with our neighbors.

We have already captured from the Holy Spirit's viewpoint some memories that open us up. When we recall these memories, our heart feels His love, peace, and joy. In healing of memories we take those memories that cripple us and look at them also from the Spirit's viewpoint.

Healing of memories happens all the time in scripture. Israel constantly goes back to its moments of slavery and wandering in the desert and senses that even in these tragic times she came closer to Yahweh. Or consider the story of Joseph sold into slavery by his brothers (Gen 45). Now this betrayal could have locked Joseph into revenge, bitterness and distrust, causing him to reject his brothers when they came to ask for food. But Joseph healed that memory. He went back and saw the redemptiveness of being sold into slavery— it placed him in Egypt so that he could feed Israel.

New Testament writers also keep asking how we are to look at events. Can we see Adam in terms of Christ, the cross in terms of resurrection? Christ's story of the lost son exemplifies the struggle running throughout scripture to look at memories from God's viewpoint so they no longer cripple us (Lk 15:11). Both the elder brother and the father look back at the same memory, namely, the younger son demanding his share of the estate and walking out on his father. Now the father goes back to that memory, takes a look at the son in front of him and says, "Yes, my son has grown a lot. Because he demanded the money and left home, he has developed in ways that he just never did around here. Let us celebrate and kill the fatted calf." On the other hand, the elder brother goes back and remembers his brother walking out and leaving him with all the work; he feels tiredness in his bones and thus resents very much the celebration. The memory that cripples the elder son and makes him resentful fills the father with hope and allows him to live with the peace and joy of the Holy Spirit.

In my own life, I thank God these days especially for my priesthood and the ability to write about the way He touches me and others through it. When I ask the Lord what He wants to heal in me, He asks that I share more, not only by writing but by sharing every facet of life.

Many past events make it more difficult for me to share. One of those events, for instance, was the way I competed with my brother to get good grades. This kept me from sharing with classmates. This basic competitive stance even today makes it hard for me to admit any ignorance, to fully profit from another's insights, or to share my own. Whatever is not healed makes it difficult to write even this book.

After I really hunger to be healed, I can ask Christ to take away the tendency to jealously compete and instead to extend the sharing love and peace of His Spirit. Besides praying and asking Christ to do this, I help by no longer merely seeing the negative effects that this painful memory inflicted on my life, but rather by seeing how it has left me with gifts and talents. For example, the same competitive drive made me apply myself more to study, made me forever grateful to God for my mind, and gave me the ability I use now to write. These and other results of God's love have gifted me with the power to grow and to change.

In healing of memories I must make a choice: Will I let past hurts control me and keep me acting in self-centered ways, or will I let the peace and love of the Holy Spirit control my future. By going back to memory after memory and turning them over to the Spirit, past hurts will no longer control me; rather, the freeing power of the Spirit will rule.

When I stop and think of the way God heals memories in scripture, I become aware of Him operating through the same patterns in my own life. True, He can heal instantly, but I find that He generally works through me and calls me to:

1. thank Him for the gifts He gives me;
2. ask the Lord what He wants to heal in me;
3. share with Christ a painful memory that keeps me from getting healed;
4. help Christ to take away hurt, anger or other feelings that close me up and help Him place in me the love of His Spirit by helping me forgive as He would those involved in the painful memory;
5. continue to help Christ take away the hurt and accept the love of His Spirit by becoming thankful for that painful memory;
6. thank God for healing and imagine myself acting in His healed way.

I find myself repeating all or some of these steps as the Spirit points out to me memories that need healing. The following six chapters suggest ways of entering into each step.

Discussion Questions

1. Do you see any similarities between the story of Joseph (Gen 45) and the story of the lost son (Lk 15)?

2. Read Luke 24:13-35. How does Christ heal the painful memories these disciples are fleeing?

Personal Reflection

1. Have you experienced the healing of a painful memory? If so, what were the steps in its healing?

III
Thanking God for
Our Gifts

When a fanatic dealt several damaging blows to Michelangelo's Pietà, the world was horrified. It surprised no one when the world's best artists assembled to refashion the disfigured masterpiece.

When sculptors arrived in Italy, they didn't begin repairing the marred face immediately. Rather they spent months looking at the Pietà, touching the flowing lines, appreciating the way each part expressed suffering yet ecstasy. Some spent months studying a single part such as the hand until finally the sculptors began to see more and more with the eyes of Michelangelo and to touch and feel as the master artist would have done. When the sculptors finally began repairing the face, the strokes belonged almost as much to Michelangelo as to themselves.

Not Michelangelo's but rather God's sculpturing hand fashioned us from soil-dust into a masterpiece which surpassed even the Pietà (Gen 2:7). It should not surprise us that God constantly refashions us—that as soon as we disfigure ourselves, He's already sculpturing the pieces back together.

When we ask for healing, we shouldn't immediate-

11

ly rush into it. Rather, we should start knowing ourselves as does our Sculptor. We don't see the depth of our need for healing until we know our infinite value. The least self-centered blow destroys more than any blow to the Pietà. "We are God's work of art created in Christ to live the good life as from the beginning He meant us to live it" (Eph 2:8). When we thank God for the gifts He gives us, we begin to see ourselves no longer from our own eyes but from His. If we know our giftedness, then we know how we require healing and thus we can become all that our Sculptor envisions.

Scripture helps us to see ourselves as our Creator sees us. For instance, the Genesis account of creation reveals how highly God values man, even to the extent of making him in the "image of God" (Gen 1:27). To focus on how we "image God," we prayerfully consider one of our senses or a part of our body and we appreciate it as the Creator does.

For example, look at your hand and stand in awe of it as a sculptor looking at the hand of the Pietà. Be with it in silence for a minute; then begin to notice its uniqueness so that you could pick it out in a photograph of many hands. Finish by just thanking God for it.

But we haven't thanked God enough for a gift such as our hand until we sense how that hand gifted others. Unlike other sculptors, Yahweh lives in the hands that He makes. To understand how He uses our hands to gift others, we need to step back and consider how others have gifted us through their hands. I find it very easy to realize how people have gifted me, but I find it a struggle to see how I have gifted others—how Yahweh touches others through me. But until I come to grips with this, I am seeing myself with only my limited vision and not with the eyes of my Creator.

Scripture passages about the gifts of the Holy Spirit put us in touch with another way of discovering our most profound gifts (Gal 5:22; 2 Pt 1:5-7). In these moments of peace, patience, love and kindness, we act and feel with God's heart. These gifts of the Spirit recall to my mind events where people have forgiven me, have shared what is happening between them and the Lord, and have given me a desire to live more for my community. They also recall times when I have gifted people in the same way.

Concentrating on our blessings might sound like a real ego trip. But we don't do it to boast of ourselves but of our Sculptor. In recalling our blessings, we are piecing together our own faith history as did Jeremiah or Isaiah during critical times.

As we capture more of our beauty, we are ready to pick up the bits and pieces and put ourselves back together as our Creator would. Thus when we ask Him to heal us, we are not just looking at the bits and pieces in our hands but rather at the masterpiece we are. We are ready to ask Him what He yearns to refashion in us and how we can enter into the work of His artistry.

Discussion Questions

1. Can a person who doesn't love himself love God?

2. How can you thank God for your talents, blessings, etc., without making it an ego trip?

3. How is the repairing of the Pietà similar to or different from God's mercy in repairing us?

Personal Reflection

1. Do the "Circle of God's Love" on page 92.

2. Is there one event during which you most felt God's love? How did you feel then? Was your experience similar to Galatians 5:23?

3. An even greater challenge is to do the "Triangle of Offering God's Love" on page 93.

IV
Ask Christ
What He Wants To Heal

Sometimes I ask to be healed for the wrong reasons. To seek healing only to live up to another's expectations or only to live with fewer tensions falls short of asking for healing because Christ wants me healed. Because He came to share friendship with me, Christ wants to heal me of anything that blocks that closeness (Jn 17:21). When I look at healing from Christ's viewpoint, I see my woundedness as it distances me and others from Christ.

For example, I frequently mistrust. When I ask to be healed of mistrust, it should not be because I get disappointed at myself or because this mistrust provokes my students. It must focus on Christ. For instance, when I am teaching, the real tragedy that mistrust inflicts is not between students and me but in making it more difficult for myself and my students to trust Christ.

I must share one healing with you. I had a note all written to a member of my department who frequently causes me grief because of tardiness in her reports. I had written a note to her with a tone of reprisal. Re-

flecting on how this note would affect my relationship
with God and hers with the Lord, I tore up the note and
left off the hurting statement.

By approaching healing from Christ's viewpoint,
my friend finds herself wanting to be healed of sarcasm
not only so that she can get along better with a member
of her department, but also that both of them might ul-
timately relate better to the Lord.

When I listen to Christ with the ear of my heart, I
frequently hear what Christ desires healed. If my basic
stance is toward Christ when I am doing His will, my
heart will feel His peace, joy, surrender and love. If I
feel turmoil, anxiety, sadness or a sense of war within
myself, this indicates that evil is fighting with my basic
stance and He must heal this area.

I can look over a day and feel peace disappear
when I do not rejoice in another's success or when I
alienate myself from people trying to help me. At
school I find myself uneasy when I cannot enjoy learn-
ing, when I study too much for a test, or when not entering sufficiently into discussions and into other people's experiences. Right now I lose my peace as I
become more concerned with finishing this book rather
than enjoying the present writing and discovering. But I
can look back over a day and sense when I did not feel
a deep peace, patience, and joy, times when I did not
deepen my relationship to Christ.

After Christ indicates what He longs to heal, pray
and ask Him what attitude He commonly finds present
when I am not close to Him. In my case, He focused
my attention on how often I prove my self-worth. My
friendship with Him diminishes when I live for what
people think about me, not what He thinks about me.

After I discover what makes me act in undesirable ways, I then talk to Him about whether or not I want to be healed. It is like the woman healed of the hemorrhage by touching Christ (Lk 8:40). Though many others in the pressing crowd touched Christ, none of the others reported themselves healed. Today sacramental theology emphasizes how Christ's power is not a magical touch but depends on the desires of the person receiving.[1] Whether 2,000 years ago, in the Eucharist, or in prayer for healing, Christ acts when we ask Him to heal us.

Do I really desire healing? The lost son could finally say that he wanted to be healed even if it meant being no longer a son but rather a slave (Lk 15:19). Am I willing to pay His price? For example, am I willing to depend less on what people think of me? That means I will sacrifice honor bestowed on me, the pats on the shoulders, the feeling of being needed, or the way I feel sorry for myself when my success falls short of another's. If I can say, "Yes, I want to be healed regardless of the price," then I am ready to take the next step.

But if I cannot say "yes," then I pray to desire healing. Frequently this desire arises when praying again on the ways He has blessed and healed me in my history. If I am in touch with that, then I must also know my sinfulness and how it spreads. My desire for recognition and power gets imitated and expanded into wars, economic imperialism and other tragic situations. I follow the Lord until I can finally say, "I want You to heal me regardless of the price."

If I can say "yes," then I should thank Christ for healing me in similar incidents. As I thank the Lord for past healing, I find myself sharing Christ's prayer of hopeful expectation for the areas of my life still dead to God, neighbor or myself.

"Father, I thank You for hearing My prayer. I know indeed that You always hear me." When He had said this, He cried in a loud voice, "Lazarus, hear! Come out!" The dead man came out, his hands and feet wrapped in grave clothes, and a cloth around his face. "Untie him," Jesus told them, "and let him go" (Jn 11:42).

Discussion Questions

1. Does every sin hurt other people besides the sinner?

2. Does every sin that hurts another also hurt that person's relationship with Christ?

3. Does every sin bring "rewards" making that sin attractive?

Personal Reflection

1. What feelings did you feel come and go today? Why?

2. What does Christ want to heal in you?

3. What "rewards" would you have to set aside if healed?

V
Share with Christ a Painful Memory That Keeps You from Getting Healed

Dick Brown stood only two feet away when a sniper's bullet struck President Kennedy in the neck. The bullet did not hit Mr. Brown but ever since that fateful day in Dallas, he awakens frequently with the Dallas nightmare and with a pain in his neck.

Painful memories wound us not only physically but also psychologically. A friend finds it nearly impossible to speak out ever since the time he was laughed at in grade school for giving the wrong answer.

For confession to physically and psychologically heal, we confess and expose for healing not only the scars but also what caused them. When we confess that we do not speak out as Christ would want us, we speak about a scar. But when we confess that we have not forgiven the person who laughed at us in grade school, we touch the cause.

A mother confessed time after time that she was impatient with her son, a wife that she never did the housework, a husband that he continually contradicted his wife. But real healing came for these individuals only after they dealt with the past memories that drove them to act that way.

The mother discovered that she acted most impatiently with her son whenever company came. This led her to understand that the real problem was not so much impatience with her son, but rather her fear of being rejected by friends if her son did not live up to their expectations. After going back with Christ to past events where people rejected her, and after forgiving them as Christ did, she found herself not only less threatened by the fear of being rejected, but also more patient in her mother-son relationships.

A depressed wife who accused herself of not adequately performing household tasks reflected back to the time she first began acting this way. She discovered a continuous pattern since her miscarriage nine years ago. Depression lessened as she shared with Christ the memory of her miscarriage and forgave with Him the religious institution that claimed her miscarriage was God's punishment.

A husband complained about always contradicting his wife even when she said good things. One day he caught himself talking back to his wife just as his mother had done to him and realized that he treated his wife just as his mother had treated him. He feared that just as his mother had not listened, neither would his wife. Before he could be open to his wife, he needed to share with Christ some of those painful moments between his mother and himself.

After finding the root memory, we share it with Christ just as did Cleopas and his companion on the road to Emmaus. Christ did not scold them for having their faces downcast. Rather than dealing with the immediate, He focused on what caused their depression.

They explained to Him the whole scene in Jerusalem, how they felt, and the consequences for the people (Lk 24:13). By talking over the event with Christ, they not only saw the event from their limited perspective, but also from His. Most importantly, they forgave as Christ did, a gut level forgiveness that brings healing. No longer did they walk with downcast faces but with burning hearts.

Like the men on the road, we speak to Christ about a memory that drives us to respond out of fear, guilt or hurt rather than responding to Him. Speaking about a crippling past memory might sound very psychological, and it is.

Just as we use medicine along with prayer to heal ourselves physically, so we use what is helpful in psychology along with prayer to heal us of fear, guilt or hurt. As we put Christ in touch with this memory, we come to grips with what needs to be forgiven from the gut level.

We may be aware of a memory that is at the root of our reactions. If not, we should not dig around looking for it. It is not a search and find exercise; rather, it is allowing the Holy Spirit to bring to our consciousness the painful memories He wishes to heal. Sometimes the Holy Spirit will show us a root memory by making us aware of when we first began acting this way, such as when the woman saw her problems stemming from a miscarriage. Other times He may show us a pattern in our unloving acts (e.g., our impatience whenever preparing for company), or He may speak to us of other people who treated us in the same unloving manner. Whatever and whenever He speaks, we listen to what He tells us about a memory that still controls us.

Perhaps we fear that the Spirit will bring forth a

memory that we had buried for a long time and would just as soon keep buried. But such a memory, though buried and unconscious, might still be festering within us, causing us to act in ways that hurt Christ.

When looking at this past memory, we do it from the viewpoint of someone even more beautiful than the Pietà. We do not look at this memory to see how terrible we are, but rather to see what blemish we can refashion with our Artist. If we are aware of a memory that mars us, let us thank the Spirit for this self-knowledge. If not, then let us share any painful memory with Christ.

In the same way that the Emmaus travelers talked over with Christ the events in Jerusalem, we talk over with Christ a memory that needs healing. We invite Him into the place, introduce Him to the people and listen with Him to what they are saying. This is not just to exercise our imaginations; rather, it serves the same purpose as prayerful contemplation when we recall persons, places and things in order to more intimately share a situation with Christ and experience Him.

For example, the husband who contradicts his wife may relive the painful memory of his mother constantly correcting him. He can remember the kids laughing at him as he told his mother he was too hot but still got bundled up in a sweater on a warm day. She never seemed to hear whatever he said, especially that they were calling him "mother's little boy" and telling him to go play with his dolls rather than play ball with them. The anger and rebellion make him turn off now not only his mother but others like her such as his wife. All that hurt, anger, loneliness, rebellion, and the urge to strike back must be handed over to Christ to heal. He hears every word—even those words expressed silently by clenched fists.

Just as the Emmaus travelers expressed the disappointment they felt, so the husband expresses how he felt about his mother and the situation. It is important for us to express to Christ how we feel about the hurt in order to begin seeing with His eyes what needs forgiveness.

Christ not only listened to the travelers' feelings, but He also responded to their needs. By letting Christ respond to whatever was lacking in a painful memory, we allow Him to continue the healing process. So, for example, as He walks with the husband through his childhood, Christ might remove the child's sweater and take time to hit some fly balls to him and his friends. Christ might speak to the child of how it takes a man's courage to endure all the mothering and loneliness. Christ must enter the scene, take the hurt, and touch the sore spots with His words and action.

The evil spirit frequently tempts us to either deny altogether such feelings as anger, sorrow, and anxiety or else to mention them only briefly before asking Christ to respond. As with the men on the road, Christ wants to give us all the time we need to get in touch with these feelings before He responds. Anger and similar feelings are neither good nor evil. It all depends on what we do with the feelings, whether we allow the feelings to open us up or to close us. It is not wrong to feel angry at getting a parking ticket but it is wrong to get even with the policeman. Scripture underlines this same distinction between neutral feelings and moral behavior, "Be angry and sin not. . . ." (Eph 4:26).

Being in touch with our anger and self-defeating feelings increases the possibility for healing because we can zero in on whether this or that situation causes such feelings and ask to have that painful memory healed. Once it surfaces, the anger and other feelings can be handed over to Christ in exchange for His feelings.

I remember a person who found herself estranged from God ever since a close friend died. This death confirmed for her that God did not care. Before her relationship with God could begin again, she found it necessary to sit in front of the Blessed Sacrament and shout angrily at the Lord as did the psalmists (Pss 2—13).

Perhaps it seems out of place to express to Christ exactly how we feel. But Christ Himself often expressed His gut level feelings to the Father in prayer. In near despair at Gethsemane He cried out to His Father to take this suffering away from Him, the cry of a man "sorrowful to the point of death" (Mk 14:35).

At death He finally yelled out, "My God, My God, why have You forsaken Me?" (Mk 15:34). In touch with His own feelings, Christ's forgiveness of the good thief came from the heart (Lk 23:39). We get in touch with our feelings only so we can forgive from the heart as Christ did.

Besides explaining the situation and their feelings, the disciples at Emmaus spoke to Christ of the consequences. The death of Jesus of Nazareth crushed their hope that the Great Prophet would set Israel free (Lk 24:21). We also acknowledge to Christ the consequences that this painful memory brought not only to ourselves but also to others. We tell Him, "Yes, I don't like what this wound did, but I accept the consequences, and I ask forgiveness."

As Christians we are called on not only to share the memory with Christ but also to forgive as He forgives, even when facing our enemy. As the men listened to Christ explain the scripture, they could begin forgiving as He had forgiven. Watch how Christ forgives you and the others in your painful memory. Perhaps He does it just by His presence, a touch, a glance, a request or a word. Christ leads us to go beyond merely accepting people and to really love them as He loves them.

Discussion Questions

1. The roots of painful memories can be found by asking questions such as when it began, whether it has a pattern, and whether I was ever treated as I am treating others. Can you think of other questions or ways to find the root memory?

2. How did Christ heal the memories of the disciples at Emmaus (Lk 23:13-35)? What else do you think He might have said or done that didn't get recorded?

3. Is anger like pain—a warning of something to be healed? How did Christ deal with anger?

Personal Reflection

1. Turn to page 94 and do steps 1 and 2 of the healing of memories square.

2. Would you enter the scene and talk to Christ about *all* the feelings—even anger?

3. Is there any pattern to the memories?

4. Can you get back to when one of these painful memories began?

VI
Replacing Hurt with Love by Forgiving Painful Memories

I remember being with a family who experienced in a few minutes the deepest anger and resentment toward each other and then the deepest love. Communication closed down when their daughter told them she would get married in four months. They knew that she could not make it financially, that if she loved them she would stay home and finish college, and that an infatuated eighteen year old was not really in love. The daughter responded that she knew she was in love and all other considerations were secondary.

For several hours a heated conversation boiled on with no listeners. They finally all gathered around and prayed with her. After prayer, even though no one changed his mind about the decision, the whole family felt a deep love for each other.

The love they felt came through forgiveness. No longer did they hold grudges against anyone whose remarks hurt them. Rather they desired to call each other closer together than they ever were. Their forgiveness said that even if no one changed his mind, they would listen to and love each other. No longer did hurt, resentment and anger engulf them; rather, a forgiving and a loving concern embraced all.

We are asking the Spirit to do the same thing with our painful memory that He did with that family. We want to uproot any hurt, anger or resentment pressuring us to act in an unloving manner and plant God's forgiving love there. We love with God's love because through the Spirit He has poured His love into our hearts (Rom 5:5).

By asking the Spirit to root out any hurt and to plant God's forgiving love, we are choosing to stop being slaves and to start becoming freed men. We are expressing our willingness to surrender to Him hurts that have controlled us and to grasp the Spirit whose love fills us with power to freely act.

As Christians, Christ always confronts us to either choose the freedom that the Spirit bestows or to continue locked in slavery (Rom 8:12; Gal 5:1). The freedom of the Spirit comes from Christ who died to free us from sin and from binding memories (Rom 6:15). Choosing Christ means that we consider ourselves dead to sin and to painful memories but alive to Christ (Rom 6:2).

If we choose Christ, we choose not to limp along crippled by sin and past hurts but to live in a radically different way. During the time of the old law, the Jews wanted to live up to the expectations of various precepts but found themselves crippled by hurts or sin and powerless to act (Rom 7). But the new law pours out the dynamic, forgiving love of the Holy Spirit that not only clarifies how to live but also grants power to live that way (Rom 8). Under the new law, the Spirit breathes into us the Father's forgiving love. We need no longer be slaves to conversations where hurt people do not listen; rather, we will be free men responding with His forgiving concern to those who speak to us.

Though the Spirit can remove immediately the anger or resentment of the painful memory and replace the hurt with God's love, He usually moves gradually as we cooperate by forgiving. Having shared the memory with Christ and having thanked Him for making it life-giving, we cooperate in surrendering the painful memory to the Spirit.

A measuring stick of how much we have cooperated in giving up the hurt and replacing it with God's love would be indicated by the degree of our Christ-like forgiveness. Each time Christ offers His Father's forgiveness, He heals the crippling, painful memory with the Father's love.

I always thought it was easy to forgive like Christ. It just meant sincerely saying, "I forgive you" and holding no grudges. I can do that, but seldom do I pardon a hurt as readily, unconditionally and totally as Christ.[1]

Christ readily forgives regardless of the cost. He would forgive sins without being asked even when the act of forgiving would result in charges of blasphemy punishable by stoning (Lk 5:17-26). His hunger to forgive made him overlook all dangers to Himself, whether from angry men ready to cast stones at an adulteress or from apostles scandalized because He spoke alone to a loose and hated Samaritan woman (Jn 8:1-11).

Christ's readiness to forgive impelled Him to forgive unconditionally. The good thief secured a ticket to heaven immediately without any condition of proving his love such as suffering in purgatory (Lk 23:39-43).

Christ makes no qualifications such as: "I will forgive you if you change, give up drinking, or apologize." Even if another does not change, we are to forgive him not seven times but seventy times seven (Mt 18:22). Christ loves more not because a person is worthy of love but because He can forgive a debt of $5000 rather than just $500 (Mk 7:41).

When change does not happen, Christ still focuses on the positive. When the rich young man turned his back, Christ "looked upon him and loved him" (Mk 10:21). Sometimes the positive limits itself to lack of ignorance and so in return for hands gouged by nails, He searches not for malice but for ignorance and screams out not in pain but in forgiveness (Lk 23:34).

When change happens, Christ celebrates that and ignores the hurt. In the story of the lost son (Lk 15:11-32), the father does not focus on the hurt and wait for an apology or even allow a confession but rather interrupts the son's planned confession (Lk 15:11-32). Seeing only the growth and blind to any past hurt, the father celebrates the return and new closeness by making the offending son more honored than ever.

Perhaps we can forgive and even treat as friends those who hurt us. But would we die for them? "Greater love than this no man has than that he lays down his life for his friends" (Jn 15:13).

It is not easy to die even for a good man—though of course for someone really worthy, a man might be prepared to die—but what proves that God loves us is that Christ died for us while we were still sinners (Rom 5:8).

But Christ's love steps beyond this, for He pours out His total life not just once but daily, "This is My Blood which is to be poured out for many for the forgiveness of sins" (Mt 26:28).

Seldom can I forgive like Christ because seldom can I honestly answer like Christ these questions: Am I ready to forgive regardless of the cost? Is my forgiveness unconditional or does it depend on another changing and becoming worthy? Am I open to all the good in him and thus find myself trying to excuse and respond in love (by prayer, care, etc.) to those who hurt me? Can I, like the lost son's father, focus not on hurt but on change and growth in both of us and therefore celebrate and give thanks? Can I try to call him closer to me than he ever was before the hurt occurred? Would I die for him? We know Christ's answers. "Do unto others as you would have them do unto you" is light years away from "Forgive as God has forgiven you" (Eph 4:32).

In order to forgive as God has forgiven us, we enter the painful scene with Christ and observe how He acts and speaks. Christ enters the memory not only to heal our sore spots with His words and touch, but also to heal those who have offended us.

Thus the husband would go back with Christ and respond to his mother, especially when she corrected or mothered her child. He would watch Christ smile, embrace or take the hand of the mother as He heals the insecurity which drove her to want to be in charge of her son. Gradually the husband will mirror Christ in forgiving, touching and speaking to the mother.

If we still find it hard to speak or act in forgiving as the Lord would, we try to dispose ourselves through prayer and activity to delve deeper into forgiveness. The Lord may gradually lead us to act more charitably toward the one causing us pain. For example, He may give the husband the strength today to call his mother, next week to visit her, and the week after to invite her for dinner.

Our power to act out forgiveness will be determined to a great extent by the kind of people we allow to enter our life and the depth at which we share ourselves with them. By sharing life more completely with people who forgive readily and who value each other as another Christ, we will find it easier to extend Christ's forgiveness.

Besides the way we respond to others, our prayer life can also determine the ease and depth at which we forgive. In addition to praying for the person who hurt us, we also pray to the Spirit to reveal our history of forgiving and being forgiven. In prayer the Spirit can also help us to be Christ-like (Mk 11:25; Mt 18:21; Lk 23:39) and search for the positive qualities in someone who has hurt us. This will be a struggle because our lack of trust blinds us from appreciating him. But if we cannot find good, we must forgive just as the Father makes His sun shine on both the good and bad (Mt 5:44). Finally, we talk to Him about the painful memory, but this time we try to see with Christ's eyes what other circumstances may have driven the one who offended us. How was he reacting to much more than us?

To forgive others as Christ does may not be an uplifting experience right away. We may grow depressed as our anger shifts blame away from others to ourselves. As we forgive and blame another less for hurting us, we tend to blame ourselves more for childishly overreacting, being so easily hurt, and failing to help those who hurt us. We may feel the desire to suffer and punish ourselves once we come across the depressing discovery that we were part of the problem if we were not part of the solution. The challenge is to take the conviction of having hurt another and turn it not into self-flagellation but into asking forgiveness of Christ and of those wronged.

During the passion many became depressed at their weakness. The apostles clung together and hid, Peter ran away crying, Judas went off to find a tree, and the good thief blamed himself but finally asked Christ for forgiveness. Those who kept hope alive and sought forgiveness came even closer to Christ. Depression invites us to depend not on our own strength but to rest in Christ's forgiving embrace.

Perhaps praying the stations of the cross or reading the passion will reveal how much Christ hungers to enter our darkness and forgive us at any cost. Because depression is a sign that we have begun to forgive, He yearns even more to forgive us if we say "yes."

Jesus freely gives the gift of forgiveness. It is up to us to accept the fullness of the gift He offers. Regardless of how much we give up the hurt and replace it with God's love, it is important to leave the memory with Him at the cross and beg Him to complete the process of forgiveness until it is just as total as that which He offered the good thief (Lk 23:39). We are ready to admit that He died on the cross to shoulder our burdens, and we are finally ready to surrender this one to Him.

Christ especially can help us to forgive ourselves and whoever hurt us as we see His view on what good came from the hurt. The men on the road gave up their hurt as they listened to Christ explain how the Messiah's death brings them new life. To find how tragedy gifts our life is like Joseph seeing that being sold into slavery allowed him to feed Israel. Similarly Paul discovered that the tragedy of Adam brings a Christ and the cross brings resurrection. After forgiving, Christ invites us not to forget the memory but to remember it with Him until, seeing it from His viewpoint, we find how even this crippling memory works out for the good (Rom 8:28).

Discussion Questions

1. Did Christ ever refuse to forgive until people had first changed, apologized, suffered, or promised never to do it again?

2. If a domineering person gets angry, what might be causing this reaction? What makes people domineering?

3. How can a person sin and yet come closer to Christ than ever? What would you tell the man who commits many sins thinking that he can ask for forgiveness and then be closer to Christ than ever?

4. What does it mean "to forgive as Christ forgives"? What do you think He might have said or done in forgiving that didn't get recorded by the gospel writers in a story like Luke 7:36-50?

Personal Reflection

1. What time did you most experience being forgiven? How did you feel?

2. When were you most able to forgive? How did you feel?

3. Turn to the healing of memories square on page 94 and do step 3. What pressures made that person the way he was when he hurt you?

4. Do step 4 on the healing of memories square. Did you speak and touch him as readily and unconditionally as Christ?

5. Do step 5. What benefits did you get from not forgiving readily and unconditionally?

VII
Replacing Hurt with Love by Becoming Thankful for a Painful Memory

Although I have applied healing of memories for many years, only last year did I discover the importance of thanking God for the way a painful memory opened me to God, neighbor, and myself. After making a retreat, I was returning to work at a psychiatric hospital when the importance of becoming thankful struck me. I finally grasped that death, loneliness, or times of injustice could bring the people on the retreat closer to God and yet bring my clients to the psychiatric hospital because what one saw as a blessing, the other saw only as a tragedy.[1]

Up to that time, in healing of memories I only shared the memory with Christ and asked Him to take any hurt and replace it with His love. But frequently nothing seemed to happen. After the retreat, I perceived that when I was finally ready not only to share the painful memory with Him but also to become thankful for it, He would help me remove the hurt and replace it with His love. He did not treat me like someone who was helpless but waited until I was ready to work with Him.

Though the Lord can heal a memory all at once,
He usually works through us and at our own speed. Instead of a sudden healing, we usually change gradually
as we become more and more thankful for the memory.
We become more healed as Christ moves with us from
one stage to another. We move from sharing with Him
what a tragedy it was to saying it is all right, and finally
to saying thanks for it. We rejoice about the event even
if it did close us off from Him, because in every event
there opens new possibilities for becoming one with
Him, our neighbor and ourselves (Rom 8:28). Despite
the sinfulness that put Christ to death, the Emmaus
travelers could rejoice that through this tragic death
Christ brought His risen life. Like the men on the road,
we become more and more healed as we listen to Christ
telling us why we can be grateful for our tragic memories.

There is no memory for which we cannot be thankful.[2] If we would write down ten of our most important
gifts and then reflect on what period of life each of
these gifts developed most extensively, we would be
surprised to see how many grew during what seemed
tragic moments. The father was surprised to discover
that when he felt most heartbroken, his relationship
with his runaway son was strengthened. Similarly, the
men at Emmaus were surprised when what they consid-
ered to be the darkest moment in their life actually
turned out to be the moment Jesus Christ seized to develop a new relationship (Lk 15 and 24).

Even if we are aware of our gifts, gratitude comes
hard if the incident is too close to us. I doubt if the father could be grateful until his lost son returned, or the
men at Emmaus until they met Christ. I doubt if Joseph could be grateful for the gifts he acquired as a

result of being sold into slavery until weeks, months, or years after his brothers sold him (Gen 45).

If closeness makes gratitude hard, take Christ back to a similar situation and find the growth. In the sixth century B.C. Deutero-Isaiah and the Judean people found themselves captive in Babylon, separated from their temple and land. To keep the Judeans from despairing, Isaiah compared their plight with that of their forefathers in Egypt seven hundred years previously. The early Jews experienced the captivity in Egypt as a time for understanding Yahweh's faithfulness and for forming the bonds of a great nation. Likewise, Deutero-Isaiah challenges the captives in Babylon to look forward to establishing a deeper relationship with Yahweh and with each other (Is 40:11; 48:10).

When we ask Christ to help us become thankful for a memory, we are requesting Him to take our focus off the temple and lost land. Instead we investigate ways in which He has pried us open to God, our neighbor and ourselves. When a painful memory helps us appreciate ourselves as the gifted art work of God, when it makes us, like Joseph, more considerate of how we can serve our people, when it gives us new vision to find God's way as did the disciples at Emmaus, then we have cooperated with Christ in uprooting the controlling hurt and planting His love.

We become more aware of ourselves as God's work of art as we become conscious of the new dimensions this painful memory developed in us. Maybe we find it difficult to speak now because students laughed at us when we gave a wrong answer. But perhaps that painful incident led us to develop new ways of communication such as writing or painting. Maybe it made us at home with reflective solitude. By knowing our gifts, we focus on how this memory created new dimensions for us.

Being laughed at by our classmates not only developed new gifts in us but also opened up new ways of relating to God. Perhaps in coming to Him without many friends, we faced Him as one poor in spirit. The beatitudes in Matthew 5 speak of different ways we meet God because of a painful memory. Perhaps the memory opened us to understand certain aspects of Christ such as His experience of being shunned by friends and stumbling alone toward death.

While on His death walk, Christ probably felt abandoned by His friends. But this feeling of abandonment only sharpened His awareness of others who felt the same way. Thus He goes out to John, to His mother, to the good thief, and even leaves us the Eucharist so that we will not feel abandoned too.

Christ will show us how the painful memory opened us to others. Just ask how we are more sensitive to the possibility of hurting others in the way someone hurt us or how we empathize with people suffering in similar circumstances. A religious sister could forgive her superior's harsh words only when she began to appreciate her gift of being compassionate, a gift she developed so she likewise wouldn't hurt others. Another woman who suffered many years from depression could forgive people who drove her toward it when she recognized that her greatest gift now was the ability to empathize with and help depressed people. Through our new gifts Christ gives us the power to overcome drives which make us act in unwanted ways. When we become more and more thankful for our gifts, we are no longer controlled by hurt, anger and resentment, but, rather, we respond to the One who has gifted us.

After Christ reveals how this memory opens us to

God, our neighbor and ourselves, we ask Him that all involved in that event might also experience growth. "If anyone sees his brother commit a sin that is not a deadly sin, he has only to pray and God will give light to the sinner" (1 Jn 5:16).

Each tragic memory presents an occasion for gratitude because it forms part of our Father's family story. As a family becomes more and more family, events that once seemed tragic become events giving life. Every family retells its stories of how son and daughter grew when undergoing a failure, suffering a disappointment, or maybe even running away from home.

A basic distinction between the Christian God and other gods is that the Christian God calls us to be part of His family. This family shares the Eucharist, derived from the passover meal which was strictly a family affair. Its sons and daughters call their God "Abba," an intimate name used by a Palestinian child toward his father.[3] As Paul says, "The Spirit you received is not the Spirit of slaves bringing fear into your lives again; it is the Spirit of sons, and it makes us cry out, 'Abba, Father' " (Rom 8:15).

As we allow Christ to show us the redemptive moments of our family story, we begin viewing our life as the Father has viewed it all along. The more we grow as family and appreciate our family story, the more we will value the way He has healed His sons and daughters. We become family as we become one in gratitude.

Discussion Questions

1. The same stresses (e.g., death, illness, any loss) can lead to mental breakdowns or else to a new experi-

ence of God's love. Why do some experience it as tragedy and others as a time of growth?

2. For Joseph of Egypt, the disciples at Emmaus and the lost son, what appeared as tragedy resulted in growth. Is this "soap opera" or true to life?

3. How can a tragedy like a death of a friend or an illness bring a person closer to his true self, God and neighbor? What keeps this from happening?

Personal Reflection

1. Write down ten of your gifts. How many grew during what seemed tragic moments?

2. Turn back to the circle and triangle of God's love (pages 92-93). Did any of these experiences of loving and being loved take place in the midst of tragedy? Why did they bring you closer to God rather than into a mental hospital?

3. Look at the healing of memories square (page 94). Are you sensitized to people who get hurt in the same way? Do you find yourself trying to avoid hurting others in the ways you have been hurt?

4. On the healing of memories square, do steps 6 and 7. Try to find at least five ways you grew from the hurt.

VIII
Thank God for Healing

Whenever someone meets the Lord, we expect change. We know people who, like the good thief or the Emmaus disciples, become new once they meet the Lord. People call these moments of rededication by different names. Charismatics often refer to it as the baptism of the Spirit.[1]

Just as the baptism of the Spirit or other rededication marks a turning point, so will healing of memories. Both create new life with the same steps as the person who repents, focuses on Christ's love, and asks Christ for new power to love God, neighbor and self. As we read the following pages where a friend reveals the new life given her by healing of memories, we may recall new life that we experienced when rededicating ourselves to the Lord.

In healing of memories we experience the Spirit present through His peace and love that replaced the hurt in the memory. Where once we felt anger, resentment, or despair, now we sense the gifts of the Spirit (Gal 5:27). As we become more aware of the Spirit's feelings, we use those feelings to guide our choices.

Healing enables me to experience peace not only about past events but also to present choices. I have learned to rely on my ability for intuition—following my "first feelings" when they correspond to the peace and love I found in healing a memory.

When we choose whatever fills us with the same peace and love that came to us in healing a memory, we will find ourselves more in touch with how the Spirit leads us. Being aware of the presence of the Spirit and making decisions based on the Spirit's feelings, we sensitize ourselves to find God in all things.[2]

Not only in decisions but also in other conscious moments of prayer, God may become more intimately present.

Some effects from healing are directly related to prayer. Healing of memories has given me again the gift of Jesus' Presence-Felt. During conscious prayer time, I have a sense of humor, awareness of incongruity to some parts of living, joy even to the point of laughter —all new in prayer. I have also come to tears more easily and to an appreciation of my emotional gifts.

Having shared our giftedness, the feelings of past memories, and forgiveness with Christ, we feel much more at home with Him during prayer.

This feeling of at-homeness with God carries over to the way we feel about ourselves.

There is a clear sense of the giftedness of my life itself. I'm presently clutching less at life and relaxing more in its loveliness. Instead of constantly doing, there is the desire and the ability to provide myself with more time for relaxation. Relaxation in His presence is my keynote. This allows me to live with broader vision in my heart.

In touch with our giftedness and the Artist's love for us,

we no longer feel the compulsion to rush around and prove ourselves.

Rather than proving ourselves, healing makes us more responsive to surrender in any way that God asks, even if it means poverty, insults, or other suffering.

The gift of healing enables me to bear additional suffering. In the past I minded suffering less if I could know its significance in my life. When I couldn't, a feeling of frustration and at times guilt came into my consciousness. In the felt experience of healing, when He calls me to serve where I'll suffer, I am less concerned about the "why" of suffering and more confident that He will bring good from it as He has done in the past.

In healing memories, we experience how God gifts us even in times of suffering, poverty, and insults. Instead of still fearing these moments, we free ourselves to follow Christ anywhere, whether through poverty or riches, through success or failure, because we have experienced how both redeem (Rom 8:35-38).

Not only does healing of memories give a sensitivity to the Spirit and impel us toward God, neighbor and self, but it frequently brings physical healing. Remember that in the Sioux sweat lodge, we not only breathed on someone's heart to remove depression or on their lips so they could speak out, but we also blew on their forehead to relieve a headache.

Like the Sioux, Christians also believe that forgiveness brings not only psychological but also physical healing. As Christ's forgiveness restored movement to the paralytic, so the Church recognizes that forgiveness restores physical health (Mk 2:1). For example, in the sacrament of the sick, the priest declares that anyone who wants physical healing should have people pray for him, that he should confess his sins, and that he will be healed (Jas 5:13). Physical healing that happens at Lourdes and Fatima can happen each time we enter deeply into forgiveness.

Charles Mayo, M.D., estimates that the spiritual and psychological factor in disease varies from 65% to 75%.[3] Thus colitis, ulcers, or a heart attack may be a physical response to a strained relationship with wife or employee.[4] In the psychiatric hospital where I worked, patients often suffered ulcers, heart attacks, fainting spells or blackouts. These symptoms would disappear as they began healing of memories. When at one with ourselves and others, we get sick less and recover faster. Forgiveness puts us back in touch with ourselves and others, many times restoring us to health. God wills that we love Him, ourselves and our neighbor. He yearns to heal us of any psychological or physical sickness that stands in the way.

When psychological or physical sickness makes us more self-centered, we can imagine God calling us to be healed as a new creation.

For everyone who is in Christ, there is a new creation. The old creation has gone, and now the new one is here. It was all God's work. It was God who reconciled us to Himself through Christ and gave us the work of handing on this reconciliation (2 Cor 5:17-19).

This new creation begins the moment we say "yes" to His way of healing. To know ourselves as a new creation, we walk with Christ through moments in our future and imagine ourselves acting in His healed way.[5] As Mark states, "Everything you ask and pray for, believe that you have it already and it will be yours" (Mk 11:24).[6] Believing that we already possess God's healing power, we fight our tendency to doubt which limits our cooperation with God's desire to heal.

Ask with faith, and no trace of doubt, because a person who has doubts is like the waves thrown up in the sea when the wind drives. That sort of person, in two minds, wavering between going different ways, must not expect that the Lord will give him anything (Jas 1:7-8).

We don't expect that healing will come in exactly the way and at exactly the time we imagined. Because Christ knows and loves us more than we know and love ourselves, we must ask for His way of healing and not dictate to Him our shortsighted way. True hope expects everything from God without binding Him in any way to meet our when, where, and how. We are like a child who keeps asking his mother for things, but the love for his mother does not depend on her catering to his wishes. The mother does only what she knows is best for the child and the child knows this. So we too walk with Christ through moments of our future to express our confidence that He will heal us in *His* ways, directing us more and more to Him in our neighbor and in ourselves.

Celebration always followed the healing of a memory. Joseph threw his arms around Benjamin and wept; the father killed the fatted calf, and the men on the road rushed off to celebrate with the apostles (Gen 45:15; Lk 15:27; 24:34). We take time to celebrate with the Lord, to enjoy Him and to thank Him for the new creation.

By thanking Him for the new creation, we declare that forgiveness, seriously entered into, brings healing His way. It is what charismatics experience in the baptism of the Spirit or the Sioux in a sweat bath. When we come in contact with the Holy One and extend His forgiveness, we have only to ask and we will be further healed.

Discussion Questions

1. How is forgiveness related to much mental and physical illness?

2. God has promised to heal when we ask but in His own time and way. Why might He heal in a different way or time than we ask?

3. What would you tell a person who feels either that God doesn't love him or else that he lacks faith because his prayer for healing wasn't answered?

4. How does imagining possible ways in which God is healing free us to allow God to heal? For years no one broke the four minute mile, and yet, once broken, many immediately ran under four minutes. Why?

Personal Experience

1. Have you ever experienced your prayer being answered in a better way than what you requested?

2. Have you experienced how you were able to do more once you could imagine yourself doing it?

3. If you feel sincerely grateful for how the Lord can heal, try offering that healing to yourself and to those you have hurt. Try the healing of memories diamond on page 96. Do it slowly over the period of a week or more.

IX
Getting in Touch
with Other Memories

Being freed from the hurt of one past memory might be like having a debt of $500 canceled. In surrendering more memories to Christ, He takes away not just a debt of $500 but of one of $5,000 or more. As Christ pointed out, the one forgiven a $5,000 debt probably will love his benefactor more than will the one forgiven $500 (Lk 7:41).

By surrendering other painful memories to Christ in the same way we offered one memory, we free ourselves to love God, neighbor and ourselves in a more complete way. We have mentioned how we get in touch with crippling memories by going back to when unhealthy behavior first began, by becoming aware of its patterns, or by remembering others who behaved toward us in the same way. In addition, recalling certain people, words, or institutions also puts us in touch with wounded memories.

When considering wounds from people, a husband may discover that to stop contradicting his wife, he first must forgive his mother for ignoring him. After surrendering to Christ various memories involving himself and his mother, he then considers other memories involving members of his family, past teachers, friends, and those with whom he lived or worked.

Sometimes words such as rejection, embarrassed, afraid, ignored, anger, ingratitude or gossip recall what we have not yet surrendered. "Rejection" might recall to a mother many memories to offer Christ before she will grow in patience toward her son.

When persons or words recall few memories to our mind, we consider institutions. We are scarred with wounds from our involvement or non-involvement in military, educational, economic, political and religious institutions. Recall the woman who could overcome a depression only after she had forgiven a religious institution that claimed her miscarriage was God's punishment.

Sometimes Christ works with us to heal something specifically such as a husband's quick tongue, a mother's impatience, or a woman's depression. But other times He calls for a more general healing, a getting in touch with everything that cripples us.

We respond to a call for general healing by giving up all the hurt we have suffered from the time we lived in our mother's womb until now. Even back in our mother's womb, having shared our mother's hormonal reaction to stress, we experienced the same hurt our mother did.

We can do general healing in many ways. We might divide our life up into periods such as childhood, adolescence, and adulthood. Then we could take a given amount of time, say a week, and get in touch with the memories in our childhood. The next week we might prayerfully consider the memories around adolescence and finally move through adulthood. It is more important to surrender totally one root memory giving rise to other memories rather than take many memories superficially. This requires taking time with each memory, walking through it with the Lord, forgiving as He does, and even becoming thankful for it. When we have finished with our whole life, we might start over or go back and spend more time with specific moments. Although some memories heal gradually, the healing will deepen each time we walk through the memory at the Lord's pace and in His shoes.

In going through our life, we come across periods when we can remember very little. When this happens, we ask God to take away any hurt which still controls us. Though we have forgotten, God remembers all the hard times we endured even when in our mother's womb (Is 48:1; Jer 1:5; Gal 1:15). When we are not aware of the hurt, we ask the Spirit to pray through us.

For when we can not choose words in order to pray properly, the Spirit himself expresses our plea in a way that could never be put into words, and God who knows everything in our hearts knows perfectly well what He means, and the pleas of the saints expressed by the Spirit are according to the mind of God (Rom 8:26-27).

As we reminisce through our history of hurts, the Spirit helps us to hand over everything to the Lord so that hurt feelings can yield to loving as intensely as God loves. We no longer cling to hurt and allow it to manipulate us, but rather the love of God impels us as it did the woman forgiven much.

She has anointed my feet with ointment. For this reason, I tell you, her sins, her many sins, must have been forgiven her or she would not have shown such great love. It is the man who is forgiven little that loves little (Lk 7:47).

By forgiving and being forgiven much, we allow the Lord to heal everything that stands in the way of His relationship with us.

Discussion Questions

1. As one memory gets healed, it affects the healing of other memories. Can you think of an example?

2. Memories are like branches of a tree—often inter-connected and leading to one main trunk or root. How do you uncover connected memories?

3. When would you use general healing rather than the specific healing of a particular memory?

4. Is it better to spend time healing one root memory totally or to cover many with less depth? Why?

Personal Reflection

1. Turn to the healing of memories square (page 94). Do persons, institutions or words remind you of an-other memory to heal? Is it closer to the root memo-ry than others in your square? Begin healing the next memory closest to the root memory.

2. Start a list of hurts experienced as a child, adoles-cent and adult. When the list starts to fill up, take an hour to begin a prayer of general healing. If you see some patterns of hurt, try specific healing on the root memories.

X
Prayer of
Healing Memories

Prayer is like getting out of bed—you know that you should but you put it off as long as you can. It becomes a little easier to get up if you can smell coffee and bacon and can think of the good things that will happen that day. The earlier chapters have described the benefits ahead if you decide to quit being immobilized by past hurts and rise up and begin a new day walking with Christ through a healing of memories. There is only one more step—doing it.

How would you pray for a healing of memories? Here is the prayer of a father who finds himself impatient at the office and not really enjoying his work.[1]

I-II "Lord Jesus, thank You for entering our time to heal it. I want to give You my time to heal. Especially I ask that You heal those parts of the past that still manipulate me so that my future might belong more and more to You.

"Help me to walk closely with You, Lord Jesus, through my past so that I might accept Your healing whenever You wish to give it. I trust that Your infinite power will refashion and heal me even though I may not immediately see it because You love me even more than I love myself. I thank You for wanting to heal me just as You healed everyone who asked.

III "As I walk through my past, Lord, I see all the ways You have shown Your love for me. Thank You, Lord, especially for my eleventh grade teacher who helped me appreciate painting and writing. I am grateful that I can pass these gifts on to my children. I have felt much closer to my children and just wanted to thank You for the healing You have done in that whole relationship. But especially, Lord, I want to walk with You through the last couple of weeks and let You show me other ways You have gifted and healed me. Let me pause now and be grateful as You show me what you have given me.

IV "Yes, Lord, You have healed me in many ways and I accept this as a sign that You want to do even more. What would You like to heal in me? Show me what You want to heal; I do not want this just to be my ego trip. As I walk through these past few weeks, tell me where I kept You from being present. What do You see?

"As I walk together with You, You seem to be most uncomfortable when I lose patience. Yes, that's when I seem to lose the peace, joy, and surrender that marks your presence. I guess it is mostly at the office, Lord, especially when the work piles up and I can't say 'no.' Is that it? Yes, there is something that tells me I have to work hard and prove myself. To whom? Myself, my peers, even You?

"That's the real tragedy, Lord. I begin to think I have to earn Your love, prove myself to You, that I have to produce or else. I make it harder for myself and also for those people at work to know You as Lover because when I try to prove myself I'm acting more out of fear than love.

"I make it difficult for us all to love each other with Your love, Lord. When I get angry at work, I know that spreads until all those around me get uptight and return home less able to care for their families.

"So, Lord, I really want this healed at whatever price I have to pay. Even if it means that I don't get promoted or that others start to think I am lazy, I still want to be healed of having to work to prove myself.

"Thank You, Lord, for the areas of my life in which You have already started this healing. As I said, I find myself much more patient with the kids, especially when they are playing loudly around the house. I even enjoy doing things with them, like that painting the other night. Somehow when I am with them, I have not felt that strong desire to prove myself. Continue that healing, and spread it to relations with other people in my life, especially with You, Lord, and with those at work. I want to enjoy being with You even more than I enjoy being with my children. Yes, I just want to be at home with You.

V "Lord, You can see into the past. What is behind this drive to prove myself? When did it start? It seems to have been with me a long time. Let's pause and look together at the years. As I look at the past with You, I see myself proving myself in my marriage, in the high school extracurriculars, in my grade school classes, in our first home when playing with my friends. Is there a pattern there? It seems to come especially when I am unsure of myself or when others are unsure of me. Lord, I hand over all those times to You when my parents, friends or classmates made me feel like I wasn't worth two cents. Move into those times and take out the hurt and pour in Your love.

"Is there any time You want especially to heal? That still is raw and bleeding? The memory, Lord, that hurts the most is when my dad ignored me and continued reading the newspaper. Help me to relive it with You that I might hand over to You all the feelings to heal. I can picture him coming home from the office, plunking down in his big red chair, reaching for the newspaper, and telling us to go outside and play so he could have a little peace. I would tell him that I would be quiet. A minute later I would get noisy again and he would tell me, louder than ever, 'That's enough. Now get outside. I am not going to ask you again.' That scared me and he never had to ask again.

"I would have liked to have torn that newspaper to shreds and once I even hid it. He always yelled at me especially and I felt like yelling back, 'I'm not the only one.' I cried because I was the only one who ever got blamed for anything. Maybe that's why I had to prove to them and to a lot of others since then that I was better. Lord, help me to pause a moment and to hand over to You all that I felt then and whatever has remained with me up to the present. Lord, I'm hurting. Would you touch me and speak to me now in the way I need a father?

VI "OK, You have it all in Your hands, Lord. Help me to go back into that scene with You and see what You would do. You seem to be smiling at me and my father. What is the other side You see? Why does he act this way? I guess it's probably not so different from why I act that way. Maybe he had a father who ignored him, and he sure did have a hard time at the office. Come to think of it, he was working a ten hour day without air conditioning and was never in too good health. He sure worked hard for his family. Lord, help me pause a moment and see the good You see in him and what pressures were hitting him.

"Lord, let me watch and see what You would say to him. You seem to be treating him like the lost son— loving him readily, totally in every way You can, and unconditionally whether he changes or not. You see his weakness as just being a sign that he needs more care and love regardless of the cost—even to the point of dying for him. I can't do that yet. Lord, help me to get in touch with the times I experienced forgiveness or could offer it. How did that feel? Help me pause and go with You to touch him and to say to him just what You want to say. What I can't say, please say for me.

VII "Thanks, Lord. I could never have forgiven him alone. With forgiveness comes a new depth of healing and growth that I believe is there even if hidden from my pride. But that growth also started at the time of the hurt just as it did for Joseph in Egypt or for the lost son.

"Help me now to give You thanks, Lord, for the ways I have grown because of the hurt. How did You use the hurt to make me closer to my real self, to others and to You? I guess being ignored by my dad did make me closer to my mother and make me try harder to please him. It kind of left him feeling a little guilty too and maybe that's why he later tried to get close to me. Thanks too for making me find support in new friends and later in prayer with You. Maybe I'm sensitive to ignoring my kids because I was ignored. Thanks too for the talents I developed in trying to prove myself. Thanks especially for the writing and painting which were concrete ways of saying 'I'm OK' and which I can share with my children to help them see how You have gifted them too. Lord, I'll pause and give You a chance to bring to my mind other ways You have gifted me through this hurt. Thanks too for all I will never see.

VIII "Lord, if You did so much healing already in the past without even being asked, what will You do with the future which You are now filling with love as You take away the hurt. I can see a little of how You love my father in the past. How do You want me to love others in the future? Like my boss? Let me watch You and ask that I can do it Your way.

"Lord, I think I now know a little of how You want to walk through my future with me. I can see my office desk with its pile of papers and yet I don't have that tight feeling that made me grit my teeth and work to prove myself. I think I can even smile at my boss and even accept another pile of papers from him. Would You accept that work, Lord, or would You show him the other work and ask what should be done first? I guess you would let him know the truth—there is enough work for four people and only one of me. It seems that part of the problem is that I never told him how much work I already had. When I imagine telling him this, he seems to understand. Maybe it will be OK, Lord, because You will be there. Help me to say what You would say and not just take the easy way out of proving my worth by silently accepting too much work until I am overextended and grouchy. Let me pause a moment to watch how You would go through a day in the office enjoying the people and work rather than just trying to get done and get home.

IX "Lord, You can do so much with just one situation. Yet we have just made a beginning. You wish to touch all of my life with Your healing power. So keep bringing to mind other painful memories that need Your healing. What other persons, whether individuals or institutions, have hurt me? What other painful words do You wish me to hear? Who hurt me so that even today I hurt You? You already brought some to mind during this prayer—proving myself in marriage, in high school extracurriculars, in grade school classes. Are there others? Which ones are deepest and need healing first? Bring them to mind that we may again go through this prayer forgiving and healing both them and myself. Thanks for today's healing which will open up new areas to be healed."

XI
Healing of Memories
and Confession

Many of us find ourselves going to confession less and less. Perhaps we wonder why we go at all.

For years confession was a painful time. I became very creative in discovering reasons to avoid it. I convinced myself that confession was meant for those in mortal sin because venial sin was forgiven the moment I was sorry. I would rather go off, pray, and tell Christ I was sorry in my own words rather than in a superficial, impersonal confession formula. God wants a change of heart and not a hurried list of sins which seemed to get repeated each confession. If confession is meant to meet Christ, I was not meeting Him in a priest who hurried me through and breathlessly rattled off his packaged advice in the same monotone for everyone. Why didn't he simply put it on tape?

How often do we rattle off the same old list of sins, hardly hear what the hurried priest mumbles, and find ourselves living no differently afterward?

If we never seriously break the ties of friendship between ourselves and God through mortal sin, we don't have to receive the sacrament of penance as long as we live. Although only those seriously breaking

friendship with God need to go, confession offers everyone power to love and grow. Confession is like nourish-
ing food or medical care—not something sought only
when facing death, but often used to sustain and speed
up the healing process.

At the very time when confession lines are dwin-
dling, psychiatrists like Dr. Karl Menninger are plead-
ing that we rediscover ourselves as sinners.[1] He argues
that to see ourselves as sinners brings psychological
health, because it declares that we are aware of the
harm we do, responsible for it, and thereby can change.
If men were aware of how they form part of the problem, became responsible, and changed, what problem
would remain? A world with racism, pollution, wars
and political corruption can only be a world that denies
sin. When we confess, we admit that we are neither a
hardened criminal insensitive to our wrongdoing nor
compulsively driven like the irresponsible, mentally ill.
Without confessionals we are left with either prisons or
mental institutions. To say "Bless me, Father, I have
sinned," is to say "Bless me, Father, I am responsible
and have hope that I can change."

But we could achieve most of what Menninger
talked about by speaking to a psychiatrist. What makes
confession special is that we don't have a therapist sit-
ting in another chair saying he accepts us and that we
can change, but rather that we have Christ not only forgiving us but also giving us His power to change (Mt
16:19; Jn 14:10-12).

Why Christ chose confession as the moment to extend most intensely His healing forgiveness, we don't
know. We do know Jesus Christ has chosen the sacrament of penance as a sensible meeting point to deepen
His life in us. Christ wants to be a Lover.

When two people love each other, they don't just think about each other. Rather they spend time together, hear how each is doing, and maybe even give gifts as a sign of the many ways they yearn to give themselves to each other. Christ has given us the priest and His words of forgiveness as signs of His concern for us. Though these sensible signs may disappear, the deeper reality of Jesus' healing presence remains in us.

By taking time to listen and speak to us, some priests make confession an encounter with the concerned Christ. But even when we can hardly hear what a hurried priest mumbles, even when sensible signs are minimal, Christ will forgive and make us new.

Many times I wanted to pray alone rather than confess to an impersonal priest. Could I really ask for forgiveness when I couldn't forgive a priest for being impersonal? Why do I have faith that Christ's power comes through a weak Infant 2,000 years ago or in mute bread today but not in a weak priest? Was I really open to Christ when I wanted Him to forgive in *my* personal way and not the way of confession He chose for the fullest, most personal forgiveness? In short, I was like the Pharisee: "Lord, I thank You that I am not a sinner like the rest of men who need confession. I am a good man wanting to talk about forgiveness personally and not through sinful confessors" (Lk 18:11-12).

Though the sensible sign of Christ's concern for us may not be found in a priest's impersonal routine, it will be found in the new strength we should experience after confession. The power of penance comes not just from responsibly speaking or feeling understood, but rather from Jesus Christ who has guaranteed to personally heal and forgive by the sacrament.

Healing of memories frequently draws us to take

advantage of the healing power of the sacrament because in memory after memory we faced how our sin
devastates not only ourselves but also others. For example, failure to love ourselves not only leads to proving ourselves by competing for grades rather than sharing information, but also spreads in other competitive
patterns until we find ourselves competing with the
Joneses for the biggest home or car. Just as pollution
spreads from a small stream to a river, our sin spreads
from ourselves to all of society. Our competition forces
others to compete or be hurt which, when carried to ex-
tremes, gives approval to build bigger missiles and fight
bigger wars to prove who is best. As we watch our sin
devastate the community, our heart should yearn to
seek forgiveness from all.

Perhaps the Secretary General of the United Na-
tions could forgive in the name of all. But we confess to
a priest because Christ empowers the priest to extend
not only the community's forgiveness but also Jesus'
forgiveness (Heb 5:1; Jn 20:22).[2] Confession acknowl-
edges that sin disrupts our relationship not only with
our neighbor but also with the Lord. Not only does our
need to prove ourselves stifle our relationship with the
Joneses, but it also harms both of our friendships with
the Lord. By always having to prove ourselves, we experience God as one who keeps accounts and who expects us to work harder and harder as if we must prove
ourselves worthy of His friendship. Confession ap-
proaches sin from Christ's viewpoint by treating the
real tragedy of sin as the distancing of ourselves and
others from the Lord.

The following sample confession could put a father
in touch with the Lord's healing forgiveness. We will
discuss later the three parts: thanking God, confessing

what Christ wants healed, and surrendering the painful memories to Christ for healing.

Bless me, Father. It has been three weeks since my last confession. I am a married man with four children. In my last confession I promised to be more patient with my family. I want to thank God for giving me patience with the kids when they kept asking what they could do. I guess I realized how when I was a kid, I always wanted my dad to do things with me. I also want to thank God for my ability to write and paint which I'm teaching my children now.

I hurt Christ in many people. I still have to grow in becoming more patient—this time with those outside my family. I think what makes me uptight is my hesitancy to speak out. I go to PTA meetings and have good things to say but just never say them. That's no good because the teachers need feedback from the parents. Then too at the office I find myself letting cutting remarks go by. They cut down one employee so much she finally had to quit. Some of that tightness comes in trying to keep up with the Joneses—like now I'm not paying enough attention to people at the office or to my friends because I have to work my head off just to make payments on the new house and car. I'm even getting uptight with God, find myself thinking I have to work hard and prove myself to God just as I do to the Joneses.

I want to turn over to Christ the roots that drive me to keep proving myself or make it difficult to speak out. Much of that drive probably comes from not appreciating myself. I want to give over to Christ all the times when my parents, friends, and classmates made me feel that I wasn't worth two cents. I think especially of many times when my dad would tell me he didn't want to talk. He wanted me to leave him alone particularly when he came home from work exhausted. Even here, I thank Christ for the healing that's already begun in those memories especially as Jesus shows me how to spend more time with my children. So I ask Christ through the healing power of this confession to forgive me and to help me forgive and heal whatever other situations have made it difficult for me to appreciate myself as Christ does. I ask Him between now and my next confession to especially help me heal whatever makes it harder for me to be patient with those outside my family.

And for my penance, I'm wondering if I could thank God for my father and write him a note this week. That is all, Father. I am sorry for these and all the sins of my past life, especially for being impatient.

THREE BASIC STEPS

Confession and healing of memories share the same three basic steps developed in previous chapters: thanking God (III, IX), confessing what Christ wants healed (IV), surrendering painful memories to Christ for healing (V, VI, VII, IX). The following pages describe how these three steps make confession an encounter with the Lord who heals.

1. *Thanking God*

Thanking God in confession is nothing new. "To confess" in the Old and New Testaments as well as in the Fathers of the Church often meant "to praise God."[3] Thus in his *Confessions* Augustine praises God for His gifts and healing. So too, only when we have declared how He has healed and gifted us can we truly look at sinfulness, our failure to respond in friendship to our giving Artist.

By thanking God for his giftedness as writer and painter and for giving him the patience now to teach these skills to his children, the father focuses not on a long list of sins but on Christ who heals. Not only does he acknowledge how Christ healed him in the past three weeks, but the father's gratitude begins to heal the painful root memory of his tired dad ignoring him after a hard day's work.

Healing comes to the father as he spots growth coming from the root memory. He appreciates not only his ability to write and paint which he developed when spoken communication with his dad broke down, but also how that incident made him more aware of his own children. When we speak with gratitude of ways in which God gifted us either in our life or since our last confession, we speak of how God continually heals us and of our confidence that He will do the same in this confession.

2. *Confessing What Christ Wants Healed*

Confessing what Christ wants healed, we don't trust in a long list of sins but in the power of Christ (IV). If Christ speaks of becoming less tense, we don't pretend we are perfect in other areas. But limited by our human energy, reform best comes when concentrating on only one area.

In confession, unless there is mortal sin, we are not worried about listing all our sins, but rather we focus on one way, a sign of where we need to repent.[4] In healing of memories we sense how one sinful pattern leads to another. Thus we expect that even though we concentrate on healing in one area, healing will happen in many areas.

Sorrow and the consequent determination to change deepens healing. Superficial healing follows contrition superficially focused on how our sin hurt us but ignoring how it hurt Christ in others.

Notice how the father confesses sin not as a quantity of actions that break a commandment (I stole five times), but rather as a stance that destroys friendship with Christ alive in others and in himself.[5] The father grasps how fear to speak out hurts not just himself but the school, office employees, friends, and even how he relates to God.

By enumerating where the tentacles of sin choke out life, the penitent alerts himself to all areas that need healing and has greater reason to be sorry and to change. Because he focuses on real situations and not on numbers of sins, he can pick out the common cause of the impatience—not appreciating himself.

3. Surrendering Painful Memories to Christ for Healing

When we surrender painful memories to Christ for healing, we give Christ the opportunity to change us. Never finding ourselves able to act differently, we could confess time after time our fear to speak out or our drive to prove ourselves. We can act differently, however, when instead of just mentioning surface sins, we surrender to Christ for healing the root that causes those sins (V, VI, VII, IX).

The father goes beyond the surface sins such as not speaking out or always needing to prove himself when he confesses one of the causal roots—that he doesn't appreciate himself. Once he discovers the root, he takes time to surrender memories to Christ. Thus in preparing for confession he surrenders memory after memory of times when parents, friends, and classmates made him feel worthless.

Surrendering painful memories to the Lord should

happen daily, even when not preparing for confession. Therefore before confession we don't strain to think of every memory we could surrender. Rather we give over to the Lord whatever the Spirit brings to mind that could still drive us compulsively.

Healing of memories takes time. But when we finish we expect to start changing.

I wanted confession to be a real, personal experience and yet didn't take the time to make confession more than a 15 minute routine. It wasn't surprising that there was little change because there was little preparation. I was interested only in exposing a list of sins and not in surrendering painful memories that made me act that way.

We expect to change because we have taken the time to hand over to the Lord not just surface sins but painful memories for Him to heal. By going to confession, we visibly express our willingness not to lug these memories around any more, and Christ declares that we can give them to Him.

SUGGESTING A PENANCE

As a sign of our willingness not to lug memories around but to forgive as Christ forgives, we can sometimes suggest a penance. It can be anything that signifies reconciliation, whether a prayer, a visit, a favor, a phone call or a letter. When the married man suggests praying for his father and writing a letter, he is trying to forgive his father as Christ forgives.

Thus the penance expresses the father's desire to forgive his father again and again regardless of the cost. He calls his dad closer to him, even if his father doesn't change. Though before confession we may have felt inadequate to act like Christ, when we seriously ask in the sacrament of penance for that power, He empowers us to begin doing just that (Jn 14:12-14; Col 3:13).

When we focus on the healing power of Christ rather than on a long list of sins, then the penance becomes a way for celebrating our newness. Rather than looking at penance as something we do because we are terrible sinners, penance becomes a grateful response to Christ for our new, healed lives.

HEALING IN PARTICULAR AND GENERAL CONFESSION

Confessing a particular area helps us get specific about how the Lord wants to change us as in the case of the father appreciating himself more. During times of major review such as retreats or preparation for the baptism of the Spirit, Christ may call for a more general healing, a surrendering of everything that cripples us. In response, we can make a general confession in which we hand over all crippling memories and ask that nothing in our past control us but rather only the power of the Spirit.

Since even in a general confession the focus shouldn't be so much on our sinfulness as on the Lord's healing power, it follows the same steps as a particular confession. After having thanked God for the gifts in our life, we surrender for healing all the memories to Christ where we hurt someone or someone hurt us. Again we expect to change because in confessing all past memories we take time to hand over to the Lord for healing not just surface sins but the roots that cause them.

In a general confession we also ask the community

and Christ to forgive us for allowing sin to spread not only through ourselves but through the community. We declare to the community that we want to choke out all the different roots which keep us from seeing our true worth, taking risks, making new friends, or appreciating our bodies as temples of the Holy Spirit. Like the woman who anointed Christ with oil, we will feel a new capacity to love because we will experience ourselves forgiven much (Lk 7:48).

HEALING IN THE NEW ORDER FOR INDIVIDUAL CONFESSION

Whether we make a particular or a general confession, we touch the healing power of forgiveness. A strong tradition of confession as healing and therapeutic weaves its way throughout the history of the sacrament of penance.[6] In the third century the people first called the priest "father" because they recognized that he gave life through the sacraments. The ancient Church in Syria reminded a bishop on the day of his ordination that he received the Holy Spirit to heal the Church by forgiving sins. Throughout its history the Church recognized its bishops and priests by their power to heal through forgiving sins.[7]

In the new order for individual confession the Church is returning to this ancient emphasis upon confession as a healing reconciliation rather than a hurried, impersonal experience of judgment. The confessor is to greet the penitent face to face with words of friendship and kindness. Then he speaks of trusting God and offers a scripture passage on God's healing mercy. Hopefully the positive emphasis on trust and rapport will lead to a deeper confession like the healing of memories exposing more than a list of sins and numbers. The personal, conversational tone continues with the penitent offered the option of expressing his sorrow not just by the traditional formula but in his own words to fit what he wishes healed. Finally the confessor lays hands upon the penitent in the traditional gesture of healing with the Spirit. All these changes indicate the Church's desire to make confession less of a hurried, impersonal routine and more of a deeper encounter with the Christ who forgives and heals memories.

Having met Christ and having been forgiven, we leave the confessional much like the woman who was forgiven much (Lk 7) or the lost son who comes back to the father (Lk 15). The new power to love that took place in the lives of people who met Christ's forgiveness takes place in our life as we meet Him person to person in confession. If confession offers forgiveness without healing, we have not yet met Christ.

Discussion Questions

1. Why are confession lines getting shorter?

2. Explain: "Without confessionals we are left with either prisons or mental institutions."

3. Why tell a priest rather than a therapist that one has sinned?

4. How can Christ use sinful, impersonal priests if we are to encounter Him in confession?

5. How does a sin like anger or a lie hurt our relationship both to our neighbor and to Christ? Is sin ever a private act that just hurts oneself and God?

6. There have been many people who have been healed physically, mentally, or spiritually but who lose their healing when they return to their environment. Why?

7. What do you like or dislike about the sample confession? How would you change it?

8. Why is it necessary to thank God before we can ask His forgiveness?

9. How can we make confession more than a list of sins and their numbers? Why do this?

10. Why do people after confession often experience little power to change?

11. Why suggest a penance? What might be a helpful penance for gossiping?

12. Why make a general confession?

13. How does the new rite for individual confession encourage healing of memories?

14. How does Luke 7:47 connect confession and healing of memories?

Personal Reflection

1. Prepare for healing your memories by the sacramental power of confession. You may find the following useful for preparing.
   (a) Sample confession (pages 64-65)
   (b) Preparation for confession (pages 89-91)
   (c) Scriptural preparation for confession (pages 85-88)
   (d) Healing of memories square and diamond (pages 94-97)
   These may reveal patterns of sin and root memories needing sacramental healing.

2. Take one vivid hurt (painful memory). How does it even today make you feel insecure? How does this insecurity lead to one or another of the seven capital sins?

3. Make a general confession using the painful memories exposed on the healing of memories square and diamond as well as the other painful memories you may have found in your childhood, adolescence and adulthood.

XII
Devilogue: Healing of Memories—15 Minutes a Day

After Pazuzu's star performance in *The Exorcist*, many other devils jealously have sought for publicity. One such devil, Screwtape II, feels that his colleagues are getting all the credit while doing none of the soul-breaking work. Although Screwtape II has a tempting schedule twenty-four hours a day, he has consented to a fireside interview to reveal his pride in thwarting those who wish to heal painful memories. Due to the fiendish language hurled at those seeking healing, parts of the following interview were censored.

Interviewer: Could you tell us why, although you come from a distinguished blue-blood line of devils, your assignment is to tempt those healing their memories?

Screwtape II: Yes, I would be proud to do so. We have been appalled at how many change for the worse and once again become committed Christians by healing their painful memories and forgiving those who have hurt them. This releases destructive energy to do good, and new freedom we don't intend to tolerate. But we are slowly developing a new arsenal of tactics against this healing.

Interviewer: Could you describe some of these new tactics?

Screwtape II: Yes, they spin off from our crash research program, R.W.G., Rededication Without God. We can't lose because we lead them to believe that either nothing happened or everything happened during a rededication like the baptism of the Spirit, or this new evil—healing of memories. Usually we just suggest that nothing happened because they still fall, have trouble praying, etc. Each of their faults proves that nothing is happening. But if those faults are disappearing, we remind them that they can't really be different or they would have changed those around them who still have great faults.

Once they bite this line, we hook them into thinking nothing happened either because they are not good enough to win God's favor or because they lack faith. Either way they give up on God and we have them. They never suspect that healing in some way always happens and it just needs time to grow gradually. Fortunately, the Enemy usually heals gradually so people don't grow proud, and we can help them overlook the gradual, little ways healing starts.

Interviewer: What happens if your people begin to see that healing has started?

Screwtape II: If that unlikely event occurs, Phase I becomes inoperable and we try Phase II. We keep them focused on all the "progress" they are making: those they can now forgive, all the growth they see coming from the hurt, the new freedom they sense, the depth in prayer and everything in their life that is going wrong and will if unchecked lead to the disaster of heaven. Then we suggest that complete healing has occurred and there is no reason for them to continue to work daily on further healing their painful memories. This betrays "a lack of faith" (we never use "presumption"). They could spend the time *better* doing something else—helping others, praying in another way, or whatever they feel should be done. These cause less havoc because there is less deep change and more evident results, an ideal brooding ground for pride or discouragement.

Interviewer: What if they keep working on the healing of painful memories?

Screwtape II: Then we focus on the *work*. Are they going to waste the rest of their lives putting out all the effort it takes to keep praying, focusing on the growth, and forgiving like Christ? This tactic works well on those who wear themselves out by prayer and forget they need rest and recreation. If they don't forget, we help them forget by reminding them how far short of Christ's forgiveness theirs falls. They forget that not their effort but Christ's fills the gap and condemns them to heaven.

Interviewer: Are there any who don't go overboard and wear themselves out but have a simple, daily method of continually healing painful memories?

Screwtape II: Yes, we are eternally researching how to destroy an invidious, fifteen minute practice called the daily healing of memories. We have managed to tag it with another name, the examen of consciousness, which makes it sound difficult and too complex to try. It will be tough to crack since this daily practice has the same powerful steps as healing of painful memories: gratitude for gifts, asking light for healing a root memory, sorrow for the harm done to Christ, forgiving like Christ, thanks for the growth from the hurt and seeing the new behavior Christ wants. Because it has six steps, we are sure to find a weakness and have several satanic strategies already developed for each step.

Interviewer: How do you lead a person astray from this daily examination or healing of memories?

Screwtape II: Please watch your language. If they are thanking God, they are already astray and heading for heaven. We have had some success in turning this fifteen minute period of prayer into a fifteen minute self-help, psychological review of the day. Rather than have them listen to Christ reviewing their day moment by moment, we have our clients focus on their own actions and not on Christ. Some have caught on, and rather than review their actions, they review how their feelings change throughout the day. They know that despite our research, we can't give any of the bad movements mentioned in Galatians 5:22-23: love, joy, peace, patience, kindness, self-control, goodness, gentleness, and faithfulness. When these movements are present, they know they are doing what Christ would do rather than what we suggest. We can't get these wondering for fifteen minutes whether they did the right thing. So we try to get them focused on the times they don't have peace and get them worried about that. A little worry will overcome a lot of peace. But if they keep checking during the day to retain their peace, we have lost them and they start to live constantly in the presence of the Enemy. That's when we have to trip them up on one of the six steps.

Interviewer: How do you trip them up on the first step, gratitude for their gifts?

Screwtape II: Gratitude is hard to crack since it has a coating of humility. So we help them see their gifts but get them to take the credit rather than to thank Christ for His stealthy work. We allow them to ask the opening questions: What did I do well today? When did I feel peace today? But we make sure they never think of "I" as their deepest self, Christ, who gives them the power to lose their souls to Him. If this doesn't work, we have some success making them believe that thanking Christ for His work is just a subtle form of pride and boasting. Naturally, if they want to be "good" they must not be proud. Fortunately, most people have a negative self-image and will find this step difficult, so we can suggest it isn't important for them and they should move right on to the next step rather than waste valuable prayer time.

Interviewer: Can you attack them again if they get to the second step, seeking wisdom for what root memory should be healed?

Screwtape II: Sure, we have developed several diabolical attacks. We can get them focusing on whether *what* they did was right and ignoring the feelings of peace, openness, and deep joy that always mark doing the Enemy's will. Next we try to get them to see many little ways we have been successful so they can ignore the major healing needed. If we can divide their energy into correcting many things rather than just one area, we can conquer. They fall more easily if they don't pray to see themselves as Christ sees them. By every means possible we keep them from asking when it started or if it has a pattern so they don't discover the root memory. If they should stumble on the root memory, that time they were hurt or hurt another, we flood them with one of our most effective feelings, anger. We can get them angry at the person who hurt them or at themselves for hurting another. Either way they miss being sorry for hurting Christ in themselves or in another.

Interviewer: What if they find one root memory they want healed and begin to feel sorrow for hurting Christ?

Screwtape II: That's seldom a problem because people don't have a sense of how something like anger spreads from one person to another. We can get them to feel they hurt just one other person, not the other persons this person also hurt in a chain reaction that went on and on throughout the years. Even if they don't glimpse this, they can be led to believe a perfect person like Christ is in heaven and not in the imperfect persons they hurt or who hurt them. But if they are obstinate and sorry for hurting Christ, we can deepen that sorrow with a dash of discouragement and get them to give up hope to change. If they keep hope to change, we suggest 10,000 changes under "zeal" (a top secret mixture of pride, envy, and jealousy) and we soon have them discouraged again at their 10,000 failures. The dangerous question "How did I hurt Christ?" must be replaced immediately with "What am *I* going to do about changing?" If we delay, they will have a chance to be really sorry and ask Christ's help to change. If they don't see the depth of their sin, they will still believe they have power to change without much help from Christ. Excuse me while I refresh myself with a tabasco cocktail. Would you like one?

Interviewer: No. Did you ever have some who took that next dangerous step and asked Christ to help them forgive?

Screwtape II: A few, but not many who go all the way and ask to forgive as readily, totally and unconditionally as Christ. Such people fortunately are as rare as ice cubes in hell and are mostly the fools who read scripture and get all those crazy, heroic ideas like being able to forgive another seventy times seven or even dying for him. It doesn't take much for us to convince them that this is melodramatic fantasy and not the real world of an eye for an eye and a tooth for a tooth where men are reformed by prison punishment and not lax, merciful courts. If you really want to "help" another, you have to be harsh on him. Spare the rod and spoil the child. It's only a sucker who can forgive seventy-seven times and be taken seventy-eight times. Don't worry, these dangerous ideas of forgiving as completely as does Christ aren't practiced anyplace but in scripture, and you know that was for another age and culture—not our own enlightened times. Even if they want to forgive as does Christ, we can blind them to how whoever hurt them was really reacting to other tensions in his life. They will never get close to Christ's "Father, forgive them, for they know not what they do." Fortunately, that happened only once.

Interviewer: But you admit that some still try to forgive as Christ forgives. How do you stop them from the greatest degree of forgiveness, thanking God for the growth that came from the hurt?

Screwtape II: So far we haven't had much trouble with this, but we are prepared. Our press agents have done a good job in circulating the belief that saints are strong, free from sin and failures. One guy we can't silence is Paul who has it straight: "My power is at its best in weakness" (2 Cor 12:9). But we quote scripture too, "Be perfect as My heavenly Father is perfect," and ignore telling them that perfection doesn't come from constant success but constantly bouncing back from weakness and sin. Weakness too often forces persons to depend more on the Enemy and less on themselves. But before that danger occurs, we lead them to see the Enemy as men who do not want to forgive a debt of 500 rather than 50. But some understand that the larger the debt to forgive, the more the Enemy can love and come closer. These we can inveigle to feel that they are taking advantage of God's mercy and therefore not really sorry and intent on changing. We have already spoken of these traps.

Even if they do glimpse some growth coming from their reaction to the hurt, we can limit the growth they will see. They can't even imagine that they become more empathetic and helpful to those suffering from a similar hurt. They usually pray more for strength or forgiveness but we have ways of making them see their halo even when it disappears. They try harder and make new friends, but we can get them proud of both of these. It's pretty easy to change that powerful question "What did

Christ accomplish?" to "What did I accomplish?"

Interviewer: You surely have plumbed the depths of hell to devise such devilish strategies. But what do you do with those few who reach the final step of trying to see how Christ wants them acting now that they are healed?

Screwtape II: Even if they have been healed by really forgiving until grateful for the growth resulting from the hurt, all is not lost. No one knows whether they are looking at themselves as they want to be or as the Enemy wants them to be. The only way to know if it is Christ's desire is to pray for guidance and to see whether peace comes as you try out the new behavior. Most people plan rather than pray, so they are no threat. We can give them one sure-fire plan after another until they are on fire with zeal leading to our fire. We avoid the dangerous plans that involve others and might give them the support of a Christian community. We get them to give up on the community by focusing on how the others haven't kept pace with their own fast spiritual growth and could hardly help them at this advanced stage.

It's a little harder to keep them from praying and discovering peace in doing what they imagine Christ wants done. We can make them think peace is a "wow" high rather than the quiet "yes" lived out with little feeling. It's the same trick we play on those who experience a high after the baptism of the Spirit or other rededication and begin to wonder why that fades. We tell them it is their fault rather than a natural reaction and a call from the Enemy to come closer and surrender even the feelings. They think this is only for mystics in the dark night of the soul.

Interviewer: How does anyone escape?

Screwtape II: Few do, yet my colleague, Pazuzu, is getting all the praise because he starred in *The Exorcist*. Everyone fears him even though for everyone he seizes by possession, we catch ten thousand by temptation. But keep that a secret. We would rather have them fear possession than temptation.

Interviewer: Why did you reveal your strategy for fighting the invidious daily healing of painful memories?

Screwtape II: We like to test our research and improve it. Furthermore, we are not worried. No one is going to believe that with just fifteen minutes at the end of the day, you can do so much. It's not that the daily healing of memories has failed. Like your Christianity, it's never really been tried.

Discussion Questions

1. Screwtape II and his partners help you see either your faults or your halos. When would he use one strategy rather than the other?

2. What are the six steps to daily healing of memories?

3. What are the strategies Screwtape II used against each of the six steps? Do any seem unclear?

Personal Reflection

1. Which of these strategies does Satan use most against you? Which does he use most effectively?

2. For one week try the 15 minute examination of consciousness to heal daily hurts.

Appendix

1. THANKS—What has Christ done for me? (Chapter III)

Ephesians 5:20	- *"Always* and *everywhere* give thanks to God. . . ."
1 Thesalonians 5:18	- "For *all things* give thanks. . . ."

2. EXAMINATION—How does Christ want me healed? (Chapter IV)

Matt 5:3-12	- To have the attitudes of the beatitudes.
Matt 5:13-16	- To be an apostle, the salt of the earth, the light of the world.
Matt 5:27-30	- To be chaste.
Matt 5:38-48	- To turn the cheek, love enemies, pray for those persecuting.
Matt 6:5-15	- To pray as in the Our Father.
Matt 6:25-34	- To trust God as do the lilies of the field.
Matt 16:24-28	- To take up the cross, to lose one's life.
Matt 25:14-30	- To develop and use the talents given.
Luke 10:29-37	- To be the Good Samaritan.
1 Cor 13:1-8	- To love in all its dimensions.

Gal 5:13-26	- To replace self-indulgence with the fruits of the Spirit.
Eph 4:25-32	- To avoid vices.
Col 3:5-17	- To avoid vice and to practice virtue.
Philip 2:1-5	- To put others first.
James 2:14-23	- To grow in faith expressed in love of neighbor and good works.
James 3:1-12	- To properly use the tongue.
Col 3:18-21	- To be the ideal family.

3. SORROW—How did it hurt Christ in me or in others? (Chapter IV)

| Matt 25:31-46 | - What you neglected to do to the least, you neglected to do unto Me. |
| Col 1:24 | - Christ still suffers in the Church and for the Church. |

4. HEALING—Why am I doing it to Christ? (Chapter V)

John 19:1-16	- Pilate manipulated by insecurity, political ambition, crowds, fear.
John 21	- Peter's pride and boasting is replaced by trust in Christ's love.
James 4:1-8	- Sin comes from desires fighting inside ourselves; give all to God.

5. FORGIVING—Can I forgive as Christ forgives? (Chapters VI and VII)

| Matt 6:12 | - Forgive us our debts, as we |

	have forgiven those who are in debt to us.
Matt 18:21	- Forgive not 7 times but 70 times 7.
Luke 15:11-32	- Forgiving as readily, totally and unconditionally as did the father to the lost son; be grateful for the growth in love.
Luke 22:34	- "Father, forgive them, for they know not what they do."
Luke 7:36-50	- Grateful for the new power to love, for the growth.
James 5:15	- The prayer of faith will save the sick man and he will be forgiven.
1 Jn 5:16	- Pray for the sinner and God will give life to the sinner.

6. CHANGING—What will I do for Christ with His power? (Chapter VIII)

Luke 9:23	- If anyone wants to be a follower of Mine, let him renounce himself, and take up his cross *every day* and follow Me.
Romans 5:20	- But however great the number of sins committed, grace was even greater.
Romans 8	- The new life possible with the Spirit.
Col 1:14	- In Him we gain our freedom, the forgiveness of sins.

87

1 Jn 1:8 - If we say we have no sin in us, we are deceiving ourselves and refusing to admit the truth; but if we acknowledge our sins then God who is faithful and just will forgive our sins and purify us from everything that is wrong.

PREPARATION FOR CONFESSION

1. THANKS—What has Christ done for me? (Chapter III)
What am I trying to do? How through Christ's help did I succeed? What signs of God's love did I experience since my last confession (people, events)? Why did things go well (rested, less tension, more prayer, positive focus, etc.)?

2. EXAMINATION—Look at the cross and ask: What have I done for Christ? (Chapter IV)
What am I trying to do? How does Christ want me further healed? What were the low points—times of tension, discouragement, boredom, hurt, etc.?

Responses to hurt:
Pride—When did I fail to see my true worth and so have to act for others, lie, judge, fail to listen, be dogmatic or touchy, ignore their successes?
What faults have I seen in others? Am I blind to my role in causing these?
Do I judge because the evil is in me or because I am proud of my strengths?
Covetousness—When do I act as if money, goods, time are mine rather than a gift?
Lust—How is each part of my body not used to love others?
Anger—What do I fear? Worry about? Resent in others? Find hard to forgive?

Have I grown from the failures, tensions, hurts?

When did I react rather than act (e.g., compete, conform)?

When do I avoid difficult persons (e.g., egotist, complainer, needy)?

Do I face my anger rather than deny it (e.g., stomach problem, laugh less)?

Gluttony—How do I escape insecurity? Too much drink, food, TV, study, work?

Envy—Do I criticize others to build myself up? Am I bored when others are praised?

Do I belittle my success to hear others remind me of it?

Do I listen just to their words or have empathy with their feelings?

Do I make new friends? Among difficult people? Faithful to friends? To God?

Sloth—Do I fail to take risks and sacrifices because I want a tension-free life?

Where do I fall into routines rather than live with a zest?

Do I learn from the past, live in the present, and plan for the future?

Do I take time to improve myself spiritually, mentally and physically?

What good do I omit doing (corporal and spiritual works)?

How do I ignore building up my family, community, church, those I meet?

What parts of my day would Christ live differently?

3. SORROW—How did it hurt Christ in me or in others? (Chapter IV)

Which of the above bothers me the most? How does

it hurt Christ in me? In others? How has it spread? Am I sorry just because it hurt me and others or because it hurt Christ too? Am I sorry to the point where I want to change, even at great effort?

4. HEALING—Why am I doing it to Christ? (Chapter V)
Am I feeling or covering any insecurity, guilt, fear, tension, failure or hostility? Why am I attracted to this action? What do I gain from it (power, popularity, etc.)? How could I have been hurt that would lead me to respond in that way? Is there any pattern to it? When did it begin? Can I give this all to Christ?

5. FORGIVING—Can I forgive as Christ forgives? (Chapter VI)
How has Christ forgiven me (unconditionally, 7 x 70 times, readily, totally)? Can I extend His forgiveness to those who hurt me? Can I see how they were reacting to other hurts or my actions and not just to me? Have I forgiven them to the point of seeing some good that came from it (e.g., empathy toward those hurt, trying harder, more trust in Christ? (Chapter VII) Do I feel toward them as Christ would? Can I say what Christ would say?

6. CHANGING—What will I do for Christ? (Chapter VIII)
Do I really believe I can be closer to Christ than ever before (e.g., do I feel like the Lost Son or Good Thief—Jn 21; Lk 7:36-50; Ps 32 and 51)? How would Christ live my life? Can I imagine myself doing the same? Feel success? Why do I want to change? How can I remind myself to change (e.g. daily denial, reward, prayer)? Can I suggest a penance (e.g. write a letter, visit, compliments, prayer theme)?

Look back on your life at the times you experienced love and growth (both good and bad times).

1. Within the circle below, write the names (initials) of 10 people through whom God loved you and called you to grow. Draw a small circle around each of these names.

2. Within the circle below, write 10 events (abbreviated) through which God loved you and called you to grow. Draw a small rectangle around each of these events.

3. Spend time in prayer thanking God for each way He loved you.

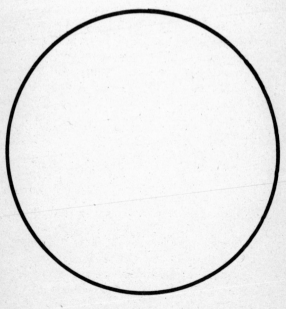

Look back on your life at the times you offered love and growth to others.

1. Within the triangle below, write the names (initials) of 10 people whom, through you, God called to love and to grow. Draw a small circle around each of these names.
2. Within the triangle below, write 10 events (abbreviate) through which God used you to call others to grow. Draw a small rectangle around each of these events.
3. Spend time in prayer thanking God for each way He used you to love others. Thank Him for how He used each part of your body. Thank Him for your corporal and spiritual works.
4. On a sheet of paper list your talents, strengths, and good points that He uses. Thank Him.

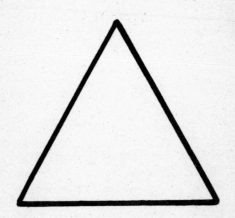

Slowly and prayerfully look back on your life at the times you were hurt.

1. Within the square write the names (initials) of 5 people who hurt you. (Think of whom you fear, avoid, judge harshly, etc.)

2. Put a circle around those who are not closer to you now. Pick one of these and tell Christ how you feel. Be honest and expose all.

3. When you can see why that person may have hurt you, put a vertical line through his name (to indicate the other pressures he faced).

4. When you feel that you can say what Christ would want to say to him, draw a horizontal line through his name.

5. When you can see that you were part of the problem and yet can forgive yourself as Christ has, make half an "X" through his name.

6. When you can see some good coming out of the hurt (at least 5 ways you grew), X it out. When you can think of some way to build a bridge to him, draw a triangle around his name. You have begun to forgive him and yourself and allow God to heal the situation.

7. Thank Christ for the growth and for beginning the healing.

8. Pick another hurt and repeat the process (be sure to add other memories to the square). Pick one that might be closer to the root memory.

9. Hand over all the situations to Christ in confession, asking for forgiveness and a healing of the relationships.

Look back at your life at the times you have hurt another.

1. Within the diamond write the names (initials) of 5 people you have hurt.
2. Put a circle around those who are not closer to you now.
3. Pick one of these. Tell Christ how you feel about hurting him. Be honest and get all the anger exposed for Christ to heal.
4. When you can figure out why you may have hurt him, put a vertical line through his name (to indicate you were not reacting just to him but to other pressures too).
5. When you feel that you can forgive both yourself and him to the degree that Christ has already forgiven both of you, draw a horizontal line through his name. Pray for a deepening of this.
6. When you can see some good coming out of the hurt (some ways both you and he grew), X out his name.
7. When you can think of some way to build a bridge to him, draw a triangle around his name. You have begun to forgive him and yourself and allowed God to enter the situation with His healing.
8. Thank Christ for the growth and for beginning the healing.
9. Add other memories to the diamond. Pick another hurt and repeat the process. Pick one that might be closer to the root memory.
10. Hand over all the situations to Christ in confession, asking for forgiveness and a healing of the relationships.

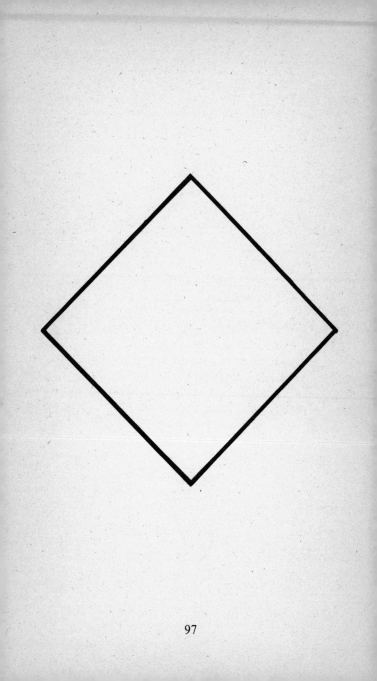

Footnotes

CHAPTER I

1. For a description of the sweat lodge ceremony cf. Ben Black Elk, *The Sacred Pipe*, Penguin Books, Baltimore, 1971, pp. 31-44.
2. For treatment of the healing of memories cf. Francis Mac-Nutt, O.P., "Inner Healing," *Pastoral Newsletter*, P.O. Box 102, Main St. Station, Ann Arbor, Michigan 48107, May, 1970; Michael Scanlon, *The Power in Penance*, Ave Maria Press, Notre Dame, 1972.

CHAPTER IV

1. Edward Schillebeeckx, *Christ, the Sacrament of the Encounter With God*, Sheed & Ward, New York, 1963.
2. For a simple updating on sacramental theology cf. Monika Hellwig, *The Meaning of the Sacraments*, Pflaum, Dayton, Ohio, 1972.

CHAPTER V

1. For exposing the root causes of sin in confession, cf. Michael Scanlon, *The Power in Penance*, Ave Maria Press, Notre Dame, 1972.

CHAPTER VI

1. For a treatment of the forgiveness of Christ, cf. James Guillet, "Jesus and Sinners," in *The Consciousness of Christ*, Newman Press, New York, 1972.

CHAPTER VII

1. For more on the steps involved in moving from viewing death as tragedy toward accepting it, cf. Elizabeth Kubler-

Ross, *On Death and Dying*, Macmillan, New York, 1970.

2. For the role of thanks in prayer, cf. Merlin Carothers, *Prison to Praise*, Logos, Plainfield, N.J., 1970.

3. For a development of the family theme in scripture, cf. David Stanley, *A Modern Scriptural Approach to the Spiritual Exercises*, Loyola Press, Chicago, 1967, p. 245.

CHAPTER VIII

1. For a survey of the charismatic movement, cf. Edward O'Connor, *The Pentecostal Movement in the Catholic Church*, Ave Maria Press, Notre Dame, Indiana, 1971. For a brief evaluation by major theologians cf. "Statement of the Theological Basis of the Catholic Charismatic Renewal," *Worship*, Vol. 47:10, Dec. 1973, pp. 610-620. For a brief explanation of the baptism of the Spirit, cf. Stephen Clark, *Baptized in the Spirit*, Dove Publications, Pecos, New Mexico, 1970.

2. For developing the practice of finding God in all things, cf. George Aschenbrenner, "Consciousness Examen," *Review for Religious*, Vol. 31:1, Jan. 1972, pp. 14-21.

3. Cited in Eugene Selzer, "Sacraments and Healing," in *Hospital Progress*, Vol. 54:10, Oct. 1973.

4. For a review of the psychosomatic dimensions of healing, cf. Morton Kelsey, "Body, Emotions and Healing," *Healing and Christianity*, Harper & Row, New York, 1973, pp. 243-277.

5. For the role of the imagination in healing, cf. Agnes Sanford, *The Healing Light*, Macalester Park Publishing Co., St. Paul, Minn., 1947.

6. The context is that we ask in Christ's name as He would for what *He* wills, not just for our limited desires. Cf. Barbara Shlemon, "Prayer for Healing," *New Covenant*, Vol. 3:5, Nov. 1973, pp. 8-10.

CHAPTER X

1. The paragraph numbers refer to the chapters which develop the thoughts within that paragraph.

CHAPTER XI

1. Dr. Karl Menninger, *Whatever Became of Sin?*, Hawthorn, New York, 1973.

2. For the role of the priest forgiving in the name of the Church, cf. Hans Küng, *The Church*, Sheed and Ward, N.Y., 1967, p. 439; Karl Rahner, *Theological Investigations*, Vol. 2, Helicon, Baltimore, 1963, pp. 135-174.

3. Jean LeClercq, "Confession and Praise of God," in *Worship*, Vol. 42:3, March 1968, pp. 169-176.

4. Karl Rahner, "Frequent Confession," in *Theological Investigations*, Vol. 3, Helicon, Baltimore, 1967, pp. 177-189.

5. For a general treatment on sin and confession, cf. Bernard Haring, *Shalom: Peace*, Farrar, Straus & Giroux, N.Y., 1967.

6. Francis Martin, "The Healing of Memories," in *Review for Religious*, Vol. 32:3, 1973, pp. 504-505; Bernhard Foschmann, *Penance and the Anointing of the Sick*, Palm Publ., Montreal, 1964, p. 120.

7. For a history of healing, cf. Morton Kelsey, *Healing and Christianity*, Harper & Row, New York, 1973, pp. 157-199.